Go Diamond!

Jan Ruhe & Jayne Leach

ISBN 0-9702667-3-1
LCCN 2003103421

Cover Design by David Anselmo with diamond from collection of Ross Andrews Goldsmith, Aspen, Colorado.

Copyright © 2003 by Jan Ruhe & Jayne Leach
Published by Proteus Press
300 Puppy Smith, Suite 205-290, Aspen, CO 81611
tel. 970-927-9380
fax 970-927-0112
www.janruhe.com
www.jayneleach.com

Dedication

To my mentors, Jim Rohn and Tom Hopkins.
To my children, Sarah, Clayton and Ashley.
To my Bill.
To all you Champion Networkers
who have been my students,
this one's for you!
-Jan Ruhe

To John, for believing in me and encouraging me
to stay true to my dreams.
My children:
Matt, for your endless big dreams, optimism
and willingness to learn.
Marcus, for paying the price and never quitting, you are a shining
example and you will be a Rugby Star.
Tabitha, for having the courage to follow your heart
and do what you love doing.
Dan, for your ability to make me laugh.
To Mum and Dad for simply being the very best
I could wish for.
You are all the wind beneath my wings,
you have kept me focused on *"Going Diamond."*
To Jan Ruhe for giving me the chance to co-author this book, thank you.
To all the rising stars in this great industry called Network Marketing,
never give up and always stay true to your dreams.
-Jayne Leach

Table of Contents

Chapter THREE:

Section 2: Train Yourself

Chapter FOUR:

Chapter FIVE:

Chapter SIX:

Chapter SEVEN:

Section 3: Train the System

What others are saying worldwide about the importance of proper training:

"I am a big believer in giving distributors strong powerful training. When a distributor feels that he/she can do the business independent of me, and they build their own successline, I know that I have done my job. The idea is to duplicate yourself over and over and let the Network Marketing explosion begin. Here is to you all going Diamond."
-Cathy Barber, The Pampered Chef, Canada

"By training, people can be changed and achieve their own goals. The time to achieve goals depends on speed of training."
-Hwang Jung Sook, Altwell Co., Royal Family, South Korea

"My business grew steadily, then in 1999 I attended a training that changed my life. I learned information contained in this book that was duplicatable. Using what I had learned and duplicating the information with my successline, my income doubled within Six months - a massive growth. This information worked for me, it will work for you."
-Dorothy Wood, Forever Living Products, Soaring Manager, UK

"Training is the way to motivate us and help to be on top. As a wild horse cannot be a fine horse without training, we should continue to train ourselves to attain a mind, attitude and behavior of successful people."
-Park Sueng Ja, Altwell Co., Royal Family, South Korea

"You are the master of your destiny. It's your choice to be successful! Going for being the best you can be means learning how to handle the gems in this book. Seize your opportunity."
-Cinnamon Harper, Regional Leader, PartyLite Gifts, Australia

"Training in Network Business is to captivate, to help, to inspire people and to develop ability to love people, so it will help to produce better results."
-Kim Shi-Joong, 'Direct Selling' Magazine, President, South Korea

"The desire to succeed combined with actions based on methods of the masters, and sprinkled with your own personality, knows no limit."
-Janet Wakeland, Independent Demonstrator, Stampin' UP! USA

"When we train we also learn...."
-Doris Wood, President of MLMIA, USA

"Joining MLM with the desire to start a business for yourself is easy but for you to be really successful in the industry, you must learn to be a professional. Is this any different from any other business venture? No it is not. To be a professional, you must learn from those who have built a business. Jan and Jayne both have. This book will help you get to Diamond too."
-Eddy Chai, Forever Living Products, Diamond, Taiwan

"Network Marketing is the opportunity to change your life. The reason why many people do not succeed even though they have lots of opportunities is that they were not trained and developed as a Networker. If you spend your time and effort to learn a successful system, developed by successful Networkers, you can achieve sincere success."
-Woo Jong Chul – International Success Science Institute, President, South Korea

" A duplicatable training is your outline for a successful future with Network Marketing. This training increased my business over 750%."
-Tara Vatske, Gold National Sales Director, PowerTeam, Discovery Toys, USA

"Read books from the people in the industry who have achieved that which you wish to achieve, and learn from them. If you put into action all that you learn, use your products, talk to people, listen to systems that get results, read books from successful networkers, and copy what works and NEVER give up, then you will Go Diamond!"
-Kim Madsen, Forever Living Products, Scandinavia

"School is never out for the pro!"
-Rita Davenport, President, Arbonne International, USA

"We tried a complicated system to get to the top position, but found that others could not follow it and do what we did, so we decided to copy those who were successful and went back to basics. Today, we use The Go Diamond System and we keep our trainings simple. With this training guide, now you can too."
-Chris and Alan Goldsbrough, Forever Living Products, UK

"Immediate training is vital to the success of new distributors. True leaders get their team on the training track the minute they sign the enrollment form. There is no better training ground than real world situations, observing presentations, attending new distributor trainings, listening to conference calls, and holding introductory shows. This gets new recruits on the road to success immediately."
-Nicki Keohohou, Direct Selling Women's Association, USA

"When it comes to training and leadership we are always reminded of the following profound philosophy. 'In order to grow, you must stay green!' This reminds us that we must always stay humble and teachable no matter how much experience we have or what lofty heights we may have already achieved. This book will enable all of us to utilize its time tested principles to reach our fullest potential in life."
-Rick and Kim Nitta, Diamonds, Forever Living Products, USA

"Education and Training are the essentials of Network Marketing. If education is to upgrade human nature, training should be based on spontaneousness."
-Kim Jung Soo, NSE Korea Co., Hawaiian Blue Diamond, South Korea

"You measure one's success by their Backbone not their Wishbone. Make a commitment to become a Master in whatever you decide to do and have a backbone to be the best trainer you can be."
-Dracy Woods, Senior Regional Vice President, PartyLite Gifts, Australia

*"Network Marketing is a simple business, if you have a **GOOD LEARNING ATTITUDE (GLA)**. Set aside your past experiences and expertise and begin to do Network Marketing as a student and learn from the Masters of the industry. Take the time to attend seminars and trainings that will further equip you with Network Marketing knowledge."*
-Edmund Ramos, Forever Living Products, Diamond, Phillipines

"Keep your trainings short and simple! Network Marketing must be easily duplicatable, and that's why it's so important to show tools, which are not complicated. Lead by example. People follow successful people. Teach distributors to follow the leader who is getting results. Don't waste time with doing everything on your own when there is already a successful leader."
-Katrin Bayri, Forever Living Products, Double Diamond, Germany

"Only one year ago our business was stagnant. We then implemented The Go Diamond System, from home, on a weekly basis. Due to this training we have watched our business grow by over 650%. This training is a simple, duplicatable way of sharing information with guests that also allows all of our team to participate - The Go Diamond System IS FANTASTIC!"
-Paul and Claire Barradell, Forever Living Products, UK

"The Go Diamond System has been instrumental in the growth of my business. It is such a simple duplicatable method of training distributors in my successline."
-Dr. Maria Idigo, Forever Living Products, Sapphire Manager, Africa

"Lifelong learning is essential for success. In this business there is no finish line. The more we learn - the more we earn."
-Pam Anders, Senior Director and Founding Consultant,
Southern Living At Home, USA

"Invest in educating yourself by attending your company's trainings, reading books written by the successful distributors in our industry, attending seminars, utilizing teleconferencing calls and finding a mentor. The return on your investment is: YOU will be the one determining your value and financial security not someone else."
-Debbi Baker, Reliv, Gold Ambassador, USA

"When you do your training, talk a lot about what it will take to reach the next level and their next pay raise (promotion). Give distributors ongoing training; and help them up the compensation plan by showing them how to train their own new distributors. The gems in this book make it all so much easier for all leaders to be Master Trainers in Network Marketing."
-Nanci Bottcher, Creative Memories, Senior Executive Director, USA

"Three basic elements in Network Marketing are selling, recruiting, and training. Training is to train how to sell products and to recruit people. Training is divided into learning, practicing, teaching, and through these processes duplication should be created. The duplication is the only way to success. There is no Network Marketing without duplication. The probability of success in Network Marketing without duplication is zero."
-Kim Tae Ho, Herbalife Korea, a member of Chairman's Club, South Korea

Diamonds are incomparable in their ability to dazzle.

The *Go Diamond* Pledge

I will act now to *Go Diamond*. I will take
action now. I will act now. From now on,
I will repeat these words each hour,
each day, everyday, until the words
become as much a habit
as my breathing. The actions I take
from here on become as instinctive as the
blinking of my eyelids. With these words I tell
myself to perform every action necessary to
Go Diamond. I will take action now. I will
repeat these words again and again and
again over and over and over. I will walk
where distributors fear to walk. I will work
when distributors seek rest. I will act now
for now is all I have. Tomorrow is the day
reserved for the labor of the lazy
distributors. I am not lazy. I will act now.
Success will not wait another minute.
If I delay, I could lose a recruit to another
and lost to me forever. This is the time.
This is the place. I am the person.
I am on fire with desire,
I am unstoppable.
Lead me, follow me or get out of my way!
I am *Going Diamond*!

The questions that people ask when starting a Network Marketing business:

What do I have to do to succeed?

Can I do it?

Will it work for me?

Is there a system I can use?

What if?

What if life was exactly as you wished?

What if people shared your excitement?

What if people shared your opinions?

What if you lived in a perfect place filled with perfect people?

What if you had no debt?

What if you had everything you wanted?

What if you could travel wherever you want, whenever you want?

What if you get the opportunity to get happily involved in Network Marketing?

What if you get into Network Marketing and don't choose to go Diamond?

What if you wake up some day and wish you had gone Diamond?

What if you get to a point in your life that you think your life is beginning to get dull?

What if for the first time in your life you decide to go for greatness and you succeed beyond your wildest expectations?

What if you can have your own identity?

What if you find a company, an opportunity that has "surprise" written all over it and you get up the courage to push the button to find that it is perfect for you?

Well, you have all that and so much more in Network Marketing! There is a day that you get in Network Marketing, but nothing happens until the day that Network Marketing gets inside of you. What if you find yourself involved in Network Marketing and feel what you feel now, think what you are thinking now and everything in your life begins to flourish and abundance and prosperity are showing up in your life...

All this happens when you decide to *Go Diamond!*

Prologue

Diamonds result in unsurpassed levels of reflection producing brilliance, fire, sparkle and light. The modern history of diamonds began in 1869 when a native boy in South Africa found a large crystal on a farm and began the dramatic rush that brought people fortunes. Diamonds have always had mystique. In South Africa, that mystique was firmly attached to the idea of power. At the head of the diamond world sat the Oppenheimer family, the richest family in South Africa. Diamond kings ruled a diamond kingdom. That was where their power lay, and the Diamond kings wanted power. In many Network Marketing companies the top position in the pay plan, the compensation plan, is called Diamond. That is where the top money earners are worldwide in Network Marketing; they are at the top position. They have gotten to the Diamond level.

Now, you have in your hands a proven and successful system to take you to the top in Network Marketing, to Diamond. This guide is in 3 parts:

How to Train Yourself
How to Train Others
Train *The Go Diamond System*

The authors of this book have achieved huge success, in two different companies in two different parts of the world and have reached the Diamond position. They have put together all of their ideas, secrets, wisdom and experience for you to ponder, debate and use. There has never been such a comprehensive Training Guide available worldwide. It will assist you in mastering training skills, so that you can build a massive business.

Here is what you will do: Start with the basics and fundamentals. Sell, sponsor/recruit others, train others, set goals, and promote up your compensation plan. Sponsor as many or as few people as you choose and when you do, you train **them** how to do the business.

Here is what to train distributors to do:

> **Use the products and love them.**
> **Share them with other people.**
> **Sponsor others into the business.**
> **Coach them how to do the same.**

This is the basic information that needs to be presented to new distributors. The more successful new distributors are from the beginning, the more orders, the more recruits, the higher the monthly activity, then the bigger their check and yours will grow. The information in this guide will provide you with options and approaches for increasing productivity. Steal one good idea…it's theft! Steal a whole bunch and it's research! Be a research pirate; there are many gems in this book for you to use.

Many people have found that they sponsored people who don't sell, don't attend meetings, don't recruit, quit and give up. Here is the reality; they were not trained with an easy, duplicatable training system. They did not know how to get started. When you have a system that works you just use it over and over again. The more trainings you do, using *The Go Diamond System* in this guide, the faster your business will grow. The outcome is that when you present *The Go Diamond System* you want your distributors to think:

"I can present that system, and I can present it better that you!"

Become a master at training others and watch your income soar to unparalleled heights. As Winston Churchill said; *"Speak to your limitations and they are yours."* There are *No Limits* on how successful you can be, except for your own limiting beliefs. **Fire Up!** Make your life an incredible masterpiece. Build a massive business. Use the system and watch your bank account grow.

Train people on all the different facets of *Going Diamond*. With the information in this guide, you can *Go Diamond* quicker than you ever believed possible. Just take action and use it. Your future starts today!

The benefits of this guide are endless. This is a trainer's guide to help you on your path to *Go Diamond*. You can train just yourself with this guide, and you can train thousands of other people now. Oh how we wish this information and road map had been available to us! We had to chart the way. Just prospect, recruit/sponsor, sell, train and help others to do the same. Savor this guide. You will refer to this guide more than any other guide in your library through the years.

The Benefits of this Guide

You Get: top tips and success methods that have been proven, giving you the security of knowing that you are using a system that lots of people have already implemented successfully.

You Get: a bridge between you and your Upline, while you are being the student, you grow your successline as you become their coach. As your business grows and duplicates, you can be sure that the correct information is taught.

You Get: a focus for all your activity in your business. You can use it in order to progressively move you from a position of relative inexperience to one of competence and confidence.

You Get: *The Go Diamond System* to use daily, weekly, monthly and year after year.

You Get: some new ideas for training yourself and others.

You Get: encouragement to use your own creative abilities. No one can make you successful. It **has** to be your choice and must come from within you.

You Get: information you need to make the transition from inexperience to being a top distributor.

You Get: to accelerate your learning curve and allow you to enjoy the rich rewards, sooner rather than later.

You Get: huge value for very little investment. What a return!

The Ten *Go Diamond* Fundamentals

Here are the basic fundamentals to *Go Diamond*. Do these over and over and over and over again for several years and you will either *Go Diamond* or be well on your way. Whenever you get off track, start over with the *Go Diamond* Fundamentals.

1. **Prospecting/Sponsoring/Recruiting**= bring in new people to your successline. Always be working on prospecting and following up and getting people happily involved in your opportunity.

2. **Use the products**= become your own best customer. Throw out all competing products. When people come to your home, have your own products in your home and life.

3. **Retail the products**= no one gets paid until product is moved.

4. **Teach others to do the same**= duplicate your efforts.

5. **Personal growth and development**= always be the student.

6. **Develop your leadership skills**= do that which you want others to do.

7. **Develop your presentation skills**= practice, drill and rehearse your presentation.

8. **Promote up your compensation plan**= always be looking at the next rung up the ladder of the plan. Don't stagnate or get content until you *Go Diamond.*

9. **Promote leaders and make *them* successful**= you want to create a lot of leaders. Invest your time in helping them succeed while you are building your personal successline.

10. **Enjoy the journey**= it's not only the money you will make; it's the person you become along the way.

Commit to Being a Master Trainer

*"Until one is committed there is hesitancy,
the chance to draw back,
always ineffectiveness.
Concerning all acts of initiative
there is one elementary truth,
the ignorance of which kills countless
ideas and splendid plans; that
the moment one definitely commits oneself,
then Providence moves too.
All sorts of things occur to help one
that would never otherwise have occurred.
A whole stream of events issues
from the decision, raising in one's favor
all manner of unforeseen incidents
and meetings and material assistance,
which no man could have dreamed
would have come his way.
Whatever you can do,
or dream you can, begin it.
Boldness has genius, power and magic in it."*
–Goethe

Section 1....
Train Network
Marketing

Introduction

When you decide that you are going to train others to succeed, the most effective way is **to be** a Network Marketer. It's best to learn the business from someone who is doing it, not from someone who has quit or *"retired"* or set themselves up as *"experts"* who have never done the business. The information in this guide comes from 100% experience in the field.

You can train one person over a kitchen table or dozens of people in a group meeting, or hundreds of people at a seminar to get massive results. It's not OK to train others to get small results. As a trainer of distributors you have a massive responsibility that you need to take very seriously to help each distributor succeed.

Here is some basic information that will help you take yourself and others to *Go Diamond*. There are *No Limits* to what you can achieve using this system. Prepare for abundance and prosperity, they are coming your way!

If we achieved Diamond status, so can you. We are not complicated women, we are not trying to entertain you, we simply want you to *Go Diamond*! Ready?

Here we grow!

 Diamond Tip: NDAOPCC = Never Do Anything Other People Can't Copy.

Chapter 1
What is Network Marketing?

Network Marketing is a true free enterprise business that offers an opportunity to build a low-start-up cost, home-based business, working around existing career and family commitments. Income can be immediate and as the business develops and grows, potentially can lead to very high long-term residual income.

It's a method of distribution, which allows independent distributors to purchase a range of high quality products direct from a company at wholesale. These products are then conversationally marketed to friends, neighbors and family at retail, as well as being used personally. This method of referral marketing is about recommending products, which the distributor personally uses and gains benefits from using. The distributor builds a business by a process of duplication, introducing and then training other people, how to do the same. The distributor is financially rewarded by the company based on a percentage of all the sales generated both by the distributor, the distributors they have sponsored, the distributors their distributors have sponsored into the business and so on. Network Marketing distributors are compensated as a result of SRL's, that's

Selling, Recruiting and Leading.

Network Marketing is when people network with their friends, family and strangers to build levels of income. The structure and marketing is the way products are distributed, but not through shops and stores. Products are distributed by many distributors within an organization selling the products to the customers.

Frequently Asked Questions

Is this one of those pyramid things? Network Marketing is a proven legal method of distribution and is not to be confused with pyramid or Ponzi schemes, or even chain letters, many of which try to pass themselves off as Network Marketing opportunities, in order to appear legal. An *illegal* pyramid scheme is an illegal business where there's a large up-front cost to join; no products or services are moved to customers; and/or where you are rewarded by a company simply for introducing someone into the program, often disguised as entrance or training fees. Such schemes are generally short lived and rely on the early entrants making lots of money at the expense of the latecomers.

What is the difference between Network Marketing and traditional companies? The difference between Network Marketing and traditional companies, is the way advertising and marketing costs are allocated. Traditional companies pay 50% or more of the final selling price of goods in advertising. They then pay salaries, commissions and benefits to marketing employees to sell products to consumers. Network Marketing companies pay those overhead costs out, by way of referral commissions, bonuses, royalties, and overrides to their network of independent self-employed distributors. It cuts out the *"middle-men."* As a distributor, you are unencumbered with traditional business headaches. Capitalization, administration, accounting, data processing, product development, purchasing, production, packaging, marketing including the design and implementation of the compensation plan, the production of sales support materials, warehousing, shipping, incentives and so much more…are all handled for you by your company. You just bring in the distributors and move the product from the company distribution center to end users!

What is the difference between Multi-Level Marketing and Network Marketing? Network Marketing is also called Multi-Level Marketing or more simply MLM, because the pay plan of commissions is based on several or multi-levels. Today, the terms Multi-Level Marketing and Network Marketing have become synonymous. It is a vast business, offering the opportunity for wealth to more people than any other form of business worldwide.

What is the difference between Network Marketing and Direct Sales? Direct Sales is a method of moving products, often door-to-door or via catalogues, where a salesperson is recruited, either as an independent or an employee, and is then rewarded based solely on the sales value of the products or services they personally sell. Network Marketing involves independent distributors, in business for themselves, who purchase products at wholesale, including for their personal use, and who are then rewarded not only for their personal sales but also on a percentage of all the sales generated by the network they have developed. They are paid on the sales of people they have sponsored, then coached and trained to build a business of their own.

Can anyone get involved in Network Marketing? Absolutely! Anyone who will enjoy the freedom to choose with whom they wish to work, which company, and what products or services they choose to represent. Anyone, from whatever background, because it's not a case of where you come from or what your background is, it's more a matter of where you want to go.

Can the ordinary person succeed? Absolutely! *The Go Diamond System* is a simple system for success, which will not fail you if you use it. It can offer the ordinary person the chance to start a business of their own from scratch, with little or no money, experience and training required. It offers a home-based or Internet based business, which can start producing an income within the first day of beginning. Network Marketing is for everyone, but not everyone is for Network Marketing.

What sort of income can I expect? It all depends on what you want. Many people join, not because they need or desire to build a business, but simply because they want to be a smart consumer, purchasing the products for themselves at wholesale. Then there are people who join for the Product Referral opportunity, still purchasing their own product usage at wholesale but covering this cost and making a small extra income of $150 to $500 (around £100 to £350) a month very part-time, conversationally marketing to friends, neighbors and family at retail. Team Builders are still part-time, usually evenings and weekends, who on top of their referral business are also involved in the sponsoring process, but not in a very large scale way. They're often happy to be making an extra $350 to $1,700 (around £250 to £1,200) a month. The **Masters** are those who are aware that incomes running into tens of thousands a month are not generated by them personally referring large quantities of product but who apply the concept of time leverage to build businesses with thousands of distributors. The really great thing is, you get to choose what income you want!

Is there still opportunity to build large successlines today?

Yes, the start of the second millennium has seen Network Marketing emerging as the most powerful distribution method for companies to move their products and services to end consumers.

Without hard work you have learned that you will never succeed. So also, without patience. Yet one may work diligently and be more patient than Job and still never rise above mediocrity unless plans are drawn and goals established. No ship ever lifted anchor and set sail without a destination. No army ever marched off to battle without a plan for victory. No olive tree ever displayed its flowers without promise of the fruit to come. It is impossible to advance properly in life without goals. Life is a game with few players and many spectators. Those who watch are the hordes who wander through life with no dreams, no goals, no plans even for tomorrow. Do not pity them. They made their choice when they made no choice. To watch the races from the stands is safe. Who can stumble, who can fall, who can be jeered if they make no effort to participate? Art thou a player? As a player ye cannot lose. Those who win may carry off the fruits of victory and yet those who are defeated, today, have learned valuable lessons that may turn the tide for them tomorrow. What do you want of your life? Consider long and well before you decide, for you may attain what you seek. Is it wealth, power, a loving home, peace of mind, land, respect, position? Whatever your goals may be, fix them in your mind and never let loose. Understand that even this may not be sufficient, for life is unfair. Not all who work hard and patiently and have goals will achieve success. Without any of these three ingredients, however, failure is a certainty. Give yourself every chance to succeed. And if you fail, fail trying! Draw up your plans today. Ask yourself where you will be, a year from today, if you are still doing the things you are doing now. Then decide where you would prefer to be in terms of wealth or position or whatever your dreams may be. Next, plan what you must do, in the next twelve months, to reach your goal. And, finally, do it!- **Og Mandino**

 Diamond Tip: Be duplicatable, it's not what you know, it's what you show.

The Benefits of the Network Marketing Industry

The benefits are endless; friendships, relationships, contacts, supplementary income, full time income, residual income and working with enthusiastic, optimistic people. Using your creativity and skills, you get the possibility of establishing and working with a group of people who have made the same commitment that you have to being massively successful and *Going Diamond*.

Why train others about the benefits of Network Marketing?

People make decisions based on the benefits to them, not for what they personally believe their needs are. Benefits must match **their** needs, not yours. To get others happily involved they must find value of what is **in it for them**. Sell the benefits of working with you, your company, the products, being a leader and the gigantic opportunity. When you come from contribution and truly want others to succeed you will take yourself out of the equation and focus on what other people want, value, and/or need.

Selling the benefits is where it all begins. When you decide to *Go Diamond*, it's because you have found the benefits for you and you have been able to share, persuade, empower, lead and enlighten others to follow you. You have sold someone the opportunity that fits their needs.

> *To sell Jane Smith what Jane Smith buys, you must see Jane Smith through Jane Smith's eyes.*

The Benefits *You Get* in Network Marketing

- **You Are** the CEO of your own organization.
- **You Can** be challenged to be your best.
- **You Can** shine as a leader.
- **You Can** talk from your heart about the products that you love.
- **You Get** a bonus check at the end of the month.
- **You Get** a business with more desirable features than any other kind of business.
- **You Get** a chance to own your life.
- **You Get** a consumable product.
- **You Get** a fabulous product range.
- **You Get** a fantastic lifestyle for your entire family.
- **You Get** a flexible way to earn income.
- **You Get** a home-based or internet based business, which can start producing an income within the first day that you start working.
- **You Get** a lifelong opportunity.
- **You Get** a possible earning from the day you join.
- **You Get** a proven method of distributing your company's products and services.
- **You Get** a quick, effective and efficient independent business with all the advantages of a small business in offering quality of service, while having the back up working with a major organization.
- **You Get** a tax shelter.
- **You Get** a title.
- **You Get** all the marketing tools you need.
- **You Get** an identity.
- **You Get** choices.
- **You Get** financial freedom in 3-5 years, if you work the program.
- **You Get** financial freedom.
- **You Get** freedom.
- **You Get** friends.
- **You Get** great confidence in yourself.
- **You Get** great recognition.
- **You Get** large pension plans.
- **You Get** lasting friendships.
- **You Get** money freedom.
- **You Get** more free time.
- **You Get** more money.
- **You Get** outstanding products.

- **You Get** paid what you are worth.
- **You Get** peace of mind.
- **You Get** personal growth and development.
- **You Get** potential.
- **You Get** pride in being part of a successful company.
- **You Get** products at a great discount.
- **You Get** rapid advancement possibilities.
- **You Get** recognition for your accomplishments and achievements.
- **You Get** residual income.
- **You Get** self satisfaction.
- **You Get** started with no qualifications.
- **You Get** started with no special degrees.
- **You Get** started with no special education.
- **You Get** the benefit of reducing taxation.
- **You Get** the chance to achieve things you may never have previously dreamed possible for yourself.
- **You Get** the chance to begin part-time.
- **You Get** the chance to build your success while empowering other people to succeed as well.
- **You Get** the chance to start from scratch, with little or no money, no precious experience needed and full training and support provided.
- **You Get** the chance to work with positive like-minded people.
- **You Get** the freedom to work the hours you choose.
- **You Get** the high esteem of the company.
- **You Get** the opportunity to create a business of your own, under the umbrella of a parent company, by building a network of distributors, through which the company's products are used and retailed.
- **You Get** the opportunity to create a lifestyle for yourself and those you love.
- **You Get** the opportunity to create massive income.
- **You Get** the opportunity to personally grow and develop.
- **You Get** the pride of being with a company that has been around a long time.
- **You Get** to accelerate your learning curve.
- **You Get** to be a part of a world-wide industry, that offers the opportunity for wealth to more people than any other form of business.
- **You Get** to be a part of the fastest growing method of distribution in the world today.
- **You Get** to be in a company that puts distributors first.
- **You Get** to be in a company with a fair compensation plan.
- **You Get** to be with a company with a track record.
- **You Get** to be your own boss.
- **You Get** to choose the people you work with.

- **You Get** to control your time.
- **You Get** to create something from nothing; networking offers true free-enterprise that allows you to achieve your dreams.
- **You Get** to earn incentive trips and see the world.
- **You Get** to get out of the house.
- **You Get** to go for greatness. Nobody can stop you.
- **You Get** to have fun.
- **You Get** to have the potential to earn rewards.
- **You Get** to meet positive people.
- **You Get** to participate in your company's incentive and rewards program.
- **You Get** to play on a level playing field. Everyone has a chance to succeed the same.
- **You Get** to start a business with a minimum initial investment.
- **You Get** to start at any age, (mainly over 18).
- **You Get** to take responsibility for your future.
- **You Get** to throw away your alarm clock.
- **You Get** to use business cards.
- **You Get** to wear whatever you want during the day.
- **You Get** to work flexible hours around your family life.
- **You Get** to work in a rapidly expanding company.
- **You Get** to work the business when you want.
- **You Get** to work with a company that has international growth.
- **You Get** to work with a company that has national growth.
- **You Get** to work with a company that has vision.
- **You Get** to work with a company that is privately held.
- **You Get** to work with people who have integrity.
- **You Get** unlimited income potential.
- **You Get** unlimited possibilities.
- **You Get** wealth creation.
- **You Have** a place to belong.

add more benefits here:

 Diamond Tip: The two words all people want to hear are *"YOU GET"*.

The Benefits of
Going Diamond

The benefits of *Going Diamond* differ from company to company. Here is what we have discovered that Diamonds get. Is it worth it to *Go Diamond*? You bet!

- **You Get** a top of the line new car every 3 years from the company.
- **You Get** ability to help others up the plan.
- **You Get** an opportunity to lead people to change their lives for the better.
- **You Get** asked to train at large events.
- **You Get** beautiful jewelry.
- **You Get** to discover the leader within you.
- **You Get** family protection plan benefits.
- **You Get** financial freedom.
- **You Get** financial rewards.
- **You Get** financial security.
- **You Get** free trips to exotic locations in the world.
- **You Get** annual profit–sharing checks.
- **You Get** great lifestyle.
- **You Get** great monthly income.
- **You Get** huge personal satisfaction and confidence.
- **You Get** limo service at convention.
- **You Get** monthly five figure income.
- **You Get** personal and leadership training stipends.
- **You Get** rebates and sales consistency bonuses.
- **You Get** reserved seating at events.
- **You Get** shopping sprees.
- **You Get** suites at convention.
- **You Get** training and development bonuses.
- **You Get** travel packages.
- **You Get** unit development bonuses.
- **You Get** yearly unit development bonuses.

The Benefits of Joining with You

Why train the benefits of joining with you?

When distributors first join, they are very eager and want to get started and need your training. They want to like and trust you and want you to see the invisible message plastered on their foreheads that says:

"HELP ME SUCCEED!"

Distributors want your attention; your knowledge and they want to feel that they have joined with someone who cares about their success. They will want to call you or email you frequently in the first few days and weeks as they get their confidence up to go share the products and opportunity with the people in their lives.

Distributors want to connect with go-getters; those who are going up the compensation plan or have massive goals to succeed. You can start the day you join prospecting and recruiting others. You don't have to wait. Just make a list of why people would want to work with you and your excitement and use those benefits in your presentations.

We took a poll worldwide, and here is what distributors reported to us: Here are the words to use to share with people you are prospecting, just how special it is to you that they *have joined with you*:

Use these words:

- *I am trustworthy, kind and enthusiastic.*
- *I am a contributor.*
- *I am a good friend.*
- *I am fun and love to laugh.*
- *I am always asking myself, "How can I add more value to my team?"*
- *I am always encouraging CANEI, (Constant And Never Ending Improvement) goal setting and coaching you to take your business a step further.*
- *I am approachable.*
- *I am available to support you with as much training and contact as you desire to reach YOUR goal.*
- *I am available via cell phone and email 24 hours a day for your questions.*
- *I am committed to being a successful leader and am taking you with me to Diamond.*
- *I am committed to excellence.*
- *I am committed to helping you and your team succeed.*
- *I am committed to helping you succeed in this business.*
- *I am committed to your success.*
- *I am duplicatable.*
- *I am endlessly supportive.*
- *I am enthusiastic.*
- *I am gracious.*
- *I am honest.*
- *I am knowledgeable about our products and eager to SHARE what I have and what I know with you.*
- *I am not a know it all; if I don't know how to answer your question, I will direct you to a resource to find it yourself.*
- *I am not just going to be a millionaire myself; I want to help others become millionaires as well, so if you want to be successful, follow me!*
- *I am online daily.*
- *I am positive.*
- *I am so busy giving recognition I don't need any myself.*
- *I am your cheerleader.*
- *I ardently desire your success.*
- *I attend meetings and keep learning.*
- *I believe in you before you believe in yourself.*
- *I BELIEVE in YOU.*
- *I believe you can do it.*

•*I can coach you via email.*

•*I can coach you via the phone.*

•*I can help you craft your vision for a fantastic future.*

•*I can help you succeed.*

•*I care about you and your family.*

•*I celebrate every advancement.*

•*I come from contribution.*

•*I do a Duplicatible training even before you get your kit.*

•*I do daily inspirational emails.*

•*I do weekly power coaching calls.*

•*I don't gossip.*

•*I dream big dreams.*

•*I encourage everyone to bring guests.*

•*I encourage people to be independent leaders.*

•*If I ask YOU to do it, I have or am doing it as well.*

•*If the person giving me advice doesn't have a proven track record, I consider that carefully before sharing what they suggest with you.*

•*If I ask you to do something, I have done it or am doing it myself.*

•*I focus on my team.*

•*I get great results.*

•*I give distributors help, support and friendship.*

•*I have a great team of fun loving people who are like-minded.*

•*I have been there, done that, and can share with you step by step how you can do it too.*

•*I have been trained by the best and I can pass that on to you.*

•*I have been trained by the best trainer in the world.*

•*I have on going training, conference calls and personal development opportunities for you.*

•*I have persistence.*

•*I help people through better health and personal prosperity and personal growth.*

•*I help you celebrate all the way to the top.*

•*I hold monthly meetings.*

•*I keep it simple.*

•*I look for only the best training and advice from others in our field so that I can share that with you.*

•*I love to laugh.*

•*I love to teach others to reach others.*

•*I make people feel good about what they are doing.*

•*I never give up.*

•*I offer great contests with great prizes.*

•I offer outstanding training with positive forward thinking people.
•I provide a great training system.
•I provide great support.
•I read books and listen to tapes and am constantly learning about Network Marketing.
•I offer outstanding training.
•I respect what you have to say.
•I send a monthly newsletter.
•I share my enthusiasm.
•I share my knowledge.
•I share your experiences.
•I show people and help them believe that although everyone leads busy lives, it is still possible to create a fantastic lifestyle working around family priorities.
•I stand behind my team as the #1 Coach.
•I stay in communication.
•I take pride in letting people know that by joining my team they will be a part of the #1 Team in our company.
•I treat each member of my team, no matter what his or her level of contribution is, the same.
•I try not to get emotionally involved, this is a business and I treat it accordingly, as if I am the CEO of my own company...my philosophy is I WILL PERSIST, I WILL SUCCEED.
•I treat it as if I have invested $60,000 instead of $150 dollars.
•I treat this as a business, not a hobby.
•I understand that MY goals and YOUR goals may be very different and I am willing to listen to what YOUR goals are and to help you make a plan to achieve them.
•I want to make a difference in your life.
•I will appreciate and recognize your efforts.
•I will be duplicatable.
•I will be there for you.
•I will be your cheerleader. I am the most enthusiastic, positive person I know, and that WILL rub off on YOU!
•I will coach you to coach others to be successful in the compensation plan.
•I will encourage you to better yourself through reading, seminars, and listening to tapes.
•I will give you business-building ideas.
•I will help you clearly to define your goals.
•I will lead you to success. Follow my coaching and you will succeed.

- *I will let you be a leader in your own right.*
- *I will listen and respect what you have to say.*
- *I will listen to you.*
- *I will never ever make you feel ignorant or stupid. You are safe with me.*
- *I will never tell you what you are doing won't work.*
- *I will not cut you off nor block you from any information, that will help you succeed.*
- *I will not encourage you to call in on calls or attend trainings that do not provide "meat" for your time.*
- *I will not give up on you.*
- *I will personally coach you and those you recruit to achieve your goals.*
- *I will return your phone calls and emails promptly.*
- *I will seek to show you, not talk at you.*
- *I will trust you and believe with all of my heart that you will succeed.*
- *I will try not to let emotions get involved; I treat this as a business.*
- *I won't block information from our upline who has gotten to Diamond.*
- *I won't let you fail.*
- *I work harder on myself than I do my business.*
- *I work with integrity and am honest.*
- *My desire is to build an organization of leaders who also build leaders so that everyone has a profitable business.*
- *My monthly newsletter is full of pictures and recognition.*
- *My motto is Together Everyone Achieves More - that's what a TEAM is all about. We work as a unit, for the betterment of society and ourselves at the same time.*
- *My teammates know that I will do what it takes to ensure their success.*
- *We are a great team.*
- *Why would people want to join MY team? Why wouldn't you?*
- *You get the benefit of my experience.*
- *You get valuable leadership training.*
- *Your time is important to me.*

Diamond Tip: It all starts with an attitude that makes you want to greet your new distributors saying: *"Welcome to our successline and my team! I can't wait for everyone to meet you at the next meeting, seminar, or convention. It's great that you are connected with me. Now, let's get you started!"*

The Benefits
of the Products

If you are a distributor of nutritional products, toys, books, software, skin care, telecommunications, candles, oils, stamps, magnets, clothes, kitchenware, housewares, jewelry, lingerie, cooking products, herbs, phone cards or any other products, a certain amount of product training is necessary. Often the company will do in-depth training. It is helpful to learn about how your products work, their benefits, the customer benefits and how to demonstrate or present them, answer frequently asked questions about them and to get people to see the value in owning them.

Learn
while
YOU
earn

It is not necessary to know all the unique benefits of your entire product range before starting to build your business. You do not have to have analysis paralysis before getting started.

Just learn the benefits of a few items, invest in some catalogs and get a stamp made with your name, phone number, email address and/or a web address on it and begin to share your opportunity. You will be amazed at your results.

What Keeps Distributors in the Business

Ask distributors in your business why they got happily involved in the first place and why they have continued to press on and stick with it. Network Marketing is multi-faceted; there is something for everyone. We asked some distributors worldwide,

"What keeps you in the business?"

Here are some of the answers we got:

- **You Get** a fun cooking experience.
- **You Get** a fun shopping experience from a catalog/brochure.
- **You Get** to accessorize your home.
- **You Get** to accessorize your wardrobe.
- **You Get** to achieve success.
- **You Get** an identity.
- **You Get** to be a leader.
- **You Get** to beautifully decorate both inside and outside your home.
- **You Get** better tasting food.
- **You Get** to be your own boss.
- **You Get** to connect generations.
- **You Get** to connect the past to the present day.
- **You Get** consumables.
- **You Get** convenience shopping.
- **You Get** to create your own relaxing atmosphere.
- **You Get** to develop your leadership skills.
- **You Get** effective products.
- **You Get** more energy.

- **You Get** to enrich your understanding.
- **You Get** exclusive products.
- **You Get** fantastic incentives.
- **You Get** to feel better.
- **You Get** to feel sexier, more attractive.
- **You Get** to feel younger.
- **You Get** to give your child an edge in school.
- **You Get** to have fun decorating.
- **You Get** to increase a child's self esteem.
- **You Get** to increase your child's vocabulary.
- **You Get** to keep food fresh, longer.
- **You Get** less pain.
- **You Get** to look better.
- **You Get** to lose weight.
- **You Get** to make money.
- **You Get** to meet wonderful people.
- **You Get** more confidence.
- **You Get** new friends.
- **You Get** no side effects.
- **You Get** passion for the business.
- **You Get** peace of mind.
- **You Get** to promote health and wellness.
- **You Get** to reach a level of success that you are satisfied with.
- **You Get** residual income.
- **You Get** safe products.
- **You Get** to save money on your telephone calls, Internet bills, long distance fees and utilities.
- **You Get** a sense of accomplishment.
- **You Get** to sleep better.
- **You Get** to slow down aging.
- **You Get** softer skin.
- **You Get** treated like gold.
- **You Get** a unique formula.
- **You Get** a versatile wardrobe.
- **You Get** to work your own hours.
- **You Get** to work out of your home.

 Diamond Tip: Sell the benefits, sell the benefits and then sell them once again.

Here is Who *Goes Diamond*

People who succeed are those who recognize the need for change. They are prepared to work on themselves, developing the qualities necessary to become successful, which in turn allows them to coach others to do the same. Distributors are some of the nicest, most fun and enthusiastic people you will ever meet! If you know people who have these qualities and values, contact them and invite them to join you.

People who are:	
• ambitious	• honest
• adaptable	• industrious
• assertive	• loyal
• caregiving	• motivated
• cheerful	• obsessive
• co-operative	• open-minded
• confident	• persistent
• disciplined	• positive
• easily coached	• participatory
• enthusiastic	• reliable
• entrepreneurial	• responsible
• energetic	• resilient
• fired up	• sincere
• friendly	• studious
• focused	• teachers
• fun	• trustworthy
• generous	• unstoppable
• hard working	• unwavering

They are people who:

- are not easily influenced by others
- are not excuse driven
- are not easily discouraged
- are big thinkers
- are self motivated
- are self-starters
- are willing to take risks
- build their personal teams
- build leaders and make them successful
- can, will and want to change
- can get over rejection easily
- can listen to others
- can practice self-control
- can converse with a stranger
- come from contribution
- don't complain
- don't like to have a boss
- don't need or want a boss
- feed their minds
- go to work on themselves
- have a vision of their success
- have confidence
- have patience
- have reasons why they are successful

- have strong beliefs
- intend to succeed
- like people
- like to lead
- like to learn
- like to risk trying new ideas
- like to share
- like to talk
- love recognition and significance
- participate in team spirit
- sell the benefits
- strive to be better every day
- take initiative
- understand that all cultures have their own opinions
- value friendship
- want a better lifestyle
- want extra money
- want to have their own time freedom
- want to personally grow
- will do whatever it takes
- will work on their skills
- won't give in or give up

Do the fundamentals:

Sell, recruit and teach others to do the same.

Who *Does Not* Go Diamond

There are many people who do not succeed. They blame the company, the compensation plan, their upline, their spouse or significant other, their parents, the government, the stock market, the area they live in, and just make excuse after excuse of why they can't succeed. Normally they give up and go forth to give Network Marketing a bad name. We know that many people **do succeed**. So what is the difference? Here are the people we have found that do not succeed:

People who are:

- complacent in life
- critical
- know it alls
- lazy
- not results oriented
- really shy and quiet and do not like to have conversations with others
- scared of success
- uninterested in learning
- quitters
- unfriendly people
- unkind

People who:

- blame others for their situation
- don't balance selling and sponsoring
- don't focus on building a personal team
- don't have a telephone
- don't have ambition
- don't have a vision
- don't have determination
- don't have the courage to be successful
- don't like people
- find fault
- give up
- go to a seminar, become addicted to the speaker but take no action
- interrupt
- make excuses why they aren't successful
- need a paycheck
- need someone else to pay them and give them benefits
- need to be told what to do on a daily basis
- only talk about themselves
- settle for what life has given them thus far
- stagnate after they reach a certain level
- wait for someone to motivate them
- want to always be right
- who don't believe it can work
- who don't like people
- who like to put others down
- won't attend seminars or read or listen to tapes
- won't take a risk

*A gem cannot be polished without friction,
nor man perfected without trials.*

 Diamond Tip: Ignorance on fire is better than
knowledge on ice.

The *Diamond*
vs.
the Unsuccessful Distributor

The Diamond thinks, *"I can, I will, I must, it's just a matter of time, I will not be denied."*
The unsuccessful distributor thinks: *"I will do the minimum to keep active."*

The Diamond looks for ways to make things happen.
The unsuccessful distributor dwells on challenges and reasons why something won't work.

The Diamond sees the opportunity in every difficulty.
The unsuccessful distributor sees the difficulty in every opportunity.

The Diamond lives in the present, they understand they can't change what happened 5 minutes ago, they press on.
The unsuccessful distributor lives in the past and dwells on past failures and challenges.

The Diamond looks for the good in others.
The unsuccessful distributor finds fault with others.

The Diamond sees possibilities.
The unsuccessful distributor sees limitations.

The *Go Diamond* Characteristics

It is easy to distinguish the future Diamonds in your organization. They are rare and they are noticeably different. They take action. They do not just talk about it, they work the business. The distributors who reach out to those getting results, and follow those who are getting results and who are building a successline are the ones most likely to *Go Diamond*. They are eager, excited, and enthusiastic and are in for the duration. They are not quitters or whiners or distributors in a funk. They take action by prospecting, recruiting and selling and teaching others to do the same. They don't just need to get their feeling of significance. They make a difference in the successline. They stand out as leaders. They go the way and show the way. Those distributors expect more and deserve more, whether those rewards take the form of a bonus, more leadership possibilities, more public recognition, or encouragement. They attend the seminars, they want to succeed, and they seek out information from those who are living the lifestyle they want to have.

Going Diamond is not a popularity contest. Trying not to offend anyone or trying to get everyone to like you, will set you on the road to being average. The average distributors hang out with mediocre people because they don't take risks. When you take risks, some people will follow you and some won't. Why? Because people who waver and procrastinate usually can't make tough choices when there is a need for one. Distributors who care more about being liked than about being effective are unlikely to confront the people who need confronting. They are unlikely to offer differential rewards based on performance. They don't challenge the status quo. And inevitably, by not challenging tradition, they hurt both their own credibility and their successline's performance.

> *Success always exacts a price which must be paid up front.*
> *If you are unwilling to pay, don't expect to achieve.*

Here is a list of characteristics that Diamond distributors have in common:

Diamonds **are:**

- **crystal clear** about the general direction in which they want to steer their successline.
- **deliberate** and methodical as they set out to spark change in their successline.
- **empathetic.**
- **experienced.** They are hard to fool; they don't react at much information they hear because they know better. They know that the best paint job can be used to hide dents and dings beneath the surface.
- **frustrated** by people with lower energy levels or those who stagnate.
- **fueled by their desire** to create and be part of a growing, thriving, successful organization.
- **good communicators** who find it fairly easy to see another person's point of view.
- **guarded** against surprises because they have been through a relentless process of digging and probing and if and when they dig and find a mess, they can acknowledge it is a mess and they can mop it up. If they dig, however, and find a Diamond, they celebrate and then they go back to digging.
- **hard** to stop once in motion.
- **high achievers.**
- **intuitive decision makers.**
- **keenly interested** in prestige and public image of their organizations.
- **masters** at delegating assignments, responsibility and authority to others.
- **not** afraid to make people angry. They don't try to make people upset but know that they can't please everyone. Even though from time to time a strong leader will upset people with their expectations and drive and changed agendas, they work hard to build a foundation for their future agendas. Diamonds are comfortable with that paradox.
- **on the go** types of people.
- **open minded.**
- **outgoing and optimistic.**
- **perceptive.**
- **risk takers.**
- **sensitive** to other's concerns, are clearly the ones in control.
- **susceptible** to becoming over-stressed.
- **team players.**
- **tenacious** in pursuit of *Going Diamond.*
- **turned on** by financial freedom.
- **very** aware that they can't please everyone all of the time.

Diamonds **ask themselves over and over**:
"What are we trying to achieve?"
"What is the outcome that I can expect if I take certain actions?"
  Once the goal is defined, they ask:
"How can I contribute to achieving these goals?"

Diamonds **have:**
- **experienced** dire situations and predictions that turn out to be the old Chicken Little warnings: The sky is falling! Very often, as it turns out, the sky isn't falling.
- a **philosophy** that they want to accomplish more than the world says is possible.

*Diamonds***:**
- **balance** that outward expression of power with a degree of patience well above that possessed by the average person.
- **bless and release** those disloyal to them with ease. They don't waste their time with critical people.
- **care** about their entire successline succeeding.
- **compromise** when necessary but there are times when they have to take action. There comes a time when they think *"I only have to do so much compromising, and then I must take action and just make the decision myself!"*
- **crave** freedom from rules; regulations, details and anything that is restricting their freedom.
- **crave** making new friends.
- **crave** meeting new people.
- **crave** new contacts.
- **develop** the best ideas.
- **deal** with disappointment fast.
- **demand** direct and to the point communication.
- **develop** the best ideas.
- **do not need** the recognition of their corporate office.
- **do not stagnate, or accept** status quo or business as usual.
- **do not want** people to be dependent upon their leadership; they want to have independent leaders so that they can enjoy the lifestyle they worked so hard to get.
- **enjoy** the challenge of getting to the top.
- **expect** to be well rewarded for their efforts.
- **feed their minds**, turn their cars into classrooms, and attend seminars taught by people more successful than they are. They build their libraries and seek out experts. They gather knowledge and can't get enough of knowledge. They are always looking for ideas.

- **find it critical** to take care of their health and well being.
- **focus** ceaselessly on making sure that their best performers are the most satisfied.
- **get products moved** through the efforts of other people.
- **generate** the most creative action plans and training systems. They implement those plans and systems better than anyone else.
- **genuinely care** about building leaders and making them successful.
- **go** to work learning all they can about people, about personalities, about exponential growth, about what the possibilities of the compensation plan are and all of the facets of the business, and will not be fooled or mislead by superficial analysis or people who tell them building a huge business can't be done.
- **hate** for people to waste their time.
- **press** on for new directions, new behaviors and new performance expectations. They push people out of their comfort zones and when those people feel too pushed, they normally take some action, which is precisely what is supposed to happen.
- **raise** the bar on performance, they spark changes, both in direction and urgency, which they understand are absolutely necessary for their successline's revitalization and success.
- **realize** that before financial success can occur, a personal growth and development program must be in place.
- **risk** enough so that enough people follow them.
- **spark** an entire successline, involving a wide variety of people, to performance.
- **spend** over their career huge amounts of time listening, learning and involving people in the change process.
- **work** hard to earn a personal commitment from distributors in their successlines.

Diamonds **have:**
- a competitive streak.
- a high level of congeniality.
- a large circle of friends and acquaintances.
- a talent and passion for being among and working with people.
- deep feelings that they want to be liked.

Diamonds **know that:**
- **gaining respect** is more important than being liked and performance is more important than popularity. Earning people's respect and being a top performer is the surest way to earn loyalty and yes, even affection.

- **it's distributors**, not comp plans, not systems, structures or budgets that make the difference between successline success and successline decline.
- **they don't attract**, retain and inspire distributors by treating everyone the same. They differentiate. This means not only rewarding top distributors but also refusing to coddle the people who don't and won't maintain their titles. They believe that ribbons, stars, medals, awards and all recognition should be reserved for the achievers.

Diamonds crave recognition in the early years:

If the top distributors don't get what they expect and deserve and have worked hard to achieve, they become deflated, de-motivated and cynical. And, they are apt to look someplace else. If they deserve recognition and are not getting it, they are ripe to leave the successline or organization and go elsewhere. They are marketable. And that can be a recipe for disaster in a successline. However, if you do give a top distributor plenty of well deserved recognition, that distributor will stay with you forever and won't go looking for some place else to get their need for significance fulfilled.

Diamonds under stress:

When under stress, Diamonds make bold leadership decisions. They do not sit on the fence. The bolder the decisions they make, the more it upsets the status quo. The more it upsets the status quo, the further likelihood that some or many distributors will get upset. But, get this…..when the successline faces turbulent and stressful times, a non-decision from the leader may very well generate more anger. If a leader does not provide the boldness and inspiration that capable distributors yearn for, the resulting disappointment they feel is enough to demoralize an entire successline. Diamonds know that when tough times come into their lives, they must make decisions. They are not afraid to make decisions. They do what they think is right at the time. Many top performers reach out to their peers during challenging times and they take the time to research all the facts before making a final decision.

Diamonds try new ideas:

If they pick up an idea from a book, a tape, a CD, a seminar or from any other source, that makes sense to them, they will try it out in their successline. Over the years, they try some ideas that work and some that don't; they add, delete or revise what they do until they find a formula that works. They do not keep doing activities that don't get results or get little to no results.

Diamonds prepare for explosive growth:

You can't get to Diamond without becoming a leader of thousands of people. Once Network Marketing kicks in, there will be explosive growth. Distributors who are *Going Diamond* need to be organized and prepare for a different life. It's a life of leadership and people needing their time. It is a life of continual challenges and navigating through and around tough times and sticking with it until you get to the Diamond level or top level of your company's compensation plan. There is no turning back for the brave. Once you take that leap of faith in yourself and your capabilities, truly, there is no stopping you. There is no stopping a person who can't be stopped.

Diamonds are always taking themselves to the next level:

Many distributors stop and stagnate along the road to Diamond. They are capable of doing more and achieving more but somewhere along the way, they make a decision that they are happy hanging out beneath the Diamond level. It's heartbreaking to watch because the Diamonds see more potential in these leaders than the leaders do. The Diamonds are always busy in strengthening the leaders who have the confidence to go to Diamond. That is where they put the majority of their efforts, time and energy. You can talk all you want for years and years that you are going to go on up the compensation plan, but at some point the Diamond realizes that it's all talk and they redirect their focus. Diamonds don't stop at Diamond. They continue to be bolder, take new directions in their lives and at some point, realize that it's of no importance to continue to get recognized year after year. They focus on how they can get their distributors to be recognized, and they work with distributors to get up the comp plan. Their focus shifts from being on themselves to ***building leaders and making them successful.***

Taking care of yourself on your rise to *Diamond*:

In *Going Diamond,* there is one major rule. You must get into a health club or spa and work out, have body work done, get enough rest, reduce the stress, take well deserved time off, have regular physicals, watch your skin, drink plenty of water, and watch your diet as you are going up the comp plan. You must, must, must take care of yourself.

> The abundance of life, the joy and the exhilaration of the Diamond lifestyle can only be found with going for it.

 Diamond Tip: Thou must take care of thyself!

"My Way" vs. *"The Diamond Way"*

Pioneers figured out long ago what works and what doesn't work. Don't try to *"reinvent the wheel."* Pioneers activity led them to finding the right formula. Simply walk in their footsteps.

What normally happens with many new distributors is that they try to find an easier and quicker *"route to the loot."* They *"try to cut corners"* and ironically, this will inevitably lengthen their journey to success. They may even give up along the way, claiming that Network Marketing doesn't work. It does but they insisted on doing it an unproven way. If you are not Diamond within a few years, you might want to try this system.

When distributors say, *"I know that is how someone else did it, but I am going to do it **my way**,"* here's what happens:

My Way:
All talk, no action... a distributor who talks a good story but never quite gets around to doing anything.

Analysis paralysis... a distributor who spends *"forever"* learning everything they feel they need to know about the products and the compensation plan before taking action.

Artificial leadership... a distributor who does not lead by example. They tell distributors to do what they are not prepared to do themselves.

Bore everyone... a distributor who believes that they need to give their prospect *"chapter and verse"* and more, in order to interest them in either the products or the opportunity.

Calls on prospects that are months old... a distributor who doesn't quite ever get around to making that call.

Calls with excuses... a distributor who always has a reason for not doing the business.

Demands... a distributor who expects more from their sponsor or the company than their own efforts deserve.

Does not attend seminars, read books, join in or listen to audio tapes... a distributor's biggest downfall. Ignorance is not bliss...whether it's from stupidity or arrogance, it will guarantee failure.

Doesn't return phone calls... a distributor who doesn't recognize that this is a relationships business. People need to talk now, not next week.

Envisions a small business... a distributor who limits not just their own growth but also that of their successline, by failing to catch the big vision and believe in it.

Expects rewards without paying the price... a distributor who wants something for nothing, never quite understanding that Network Marketing can give in three to four years, what most jobs fail to deliver in a working lifetime. The only place where *"Success"* comes before *"Work"* is in the dictionary.

Gossips... a distributor who continually *"hangs out"* with other gossiping distributors, always condemning, complaining and criticizing others.

Has an ego mentality... a distributor who has a big ego but no humility.

Has no clearly defined why... a distributor who refuses to accept the need for clearly defined, written down goals.

Is limited by the past... a distributor who uses any and every event from their past life as an excuse for not doing what they should be doing now.

Is stubborn and wants to reinvent the wheel... a distributor who is going to fail.

Isn't on the Internet... a distributor who ignores the Internet at their financial peril.

Let's their Upline do most of the work... a distributor who doesn't realize that their Upline is there to help them build a business, not there to build a business for them.

Listens to those who are not at the top... a distributor who takes advice from those who haven't done it!

Listens to those who have quit... a distributor who feels *"deep down"* that they will also fail and is looking for an alibi.

Manipulates... a distributor who has yet to realize the difference between manipulation and cooperation.

Meeeeeeeeeeeeee... a distributor who only thinks about themselves, rather than being concerned about the wants and needs of others.

Misquotes to their advantage... a distributor who tries to impress by over exaggeration, never feeling the truth is enough.

More concerned with what others do... a distributor who needs to mind their own business.

Part of the challenge... a distributor who has yet to realize, that they need to be part of the solution, not the problem.

Prospects with talking only... a distributor who won't accept that a *"picture is worth a thousand words."*

Results... a distributor who needs to realize that they are judged by what they achieve, not who they are or what they say.

Says, *"I know"* a lot... a distributor who is generally not doing, that which they claim to know.

Signs people up and uses a training that does not get results... a distributor who has failed to realize that success comes from applying a simple duplicatable training system. Diamonds don't get there by accident.

Signs up anyone who comes along... a distributor who does not realize that you need quality people to build a quality business.

Talks rather than listens to those who have the big results... a distributor who has two ears, one mouth and who hasn't yet learned to use them in that ratio.

Talks while the True Leader is making a presentation... a distributor who *"knows it all"* and is selfish enough to deprive other people of valuable information.

Unwilling to change... a distributor who won't accept that whatever they have failed to achieve so far in their life is due to their past actions.

Waiting for their spouse to... a distributor who fails to take personal responsibility.

Won't get on voicemail... a distributor who is missing a great way to communicate.

Works business one day then takes ten off... a distributor who does not recognize the need for consistent activity.

Works hard... a distributor who is half right. The second half is to work smart.

When distributors say, *"I know what the successful people have done and I'm going to do it **the proven way,**"* here's what shows up:

The Diamond Way:

All action, no talk... a distributor who realizes this business is about doing and doing it now! Massive action means massive results.

Attends the right events... a distributor who realizes the importance of attending all the events that can give them the right information to get to Diamond.

Can bless and release with ease... a distributor coaches others to be champions and leaders and then releases them to get on with building their own business.

Chooses to listen... a distributor who has two ears, one mouth and who has learned to use them in that ratio, asking questions from those who have gotten mega results, listening to the answers and then applying what they have learned.

Copies successful people... a distributor who watches the habits of successful leaders and achievers and follows their example.

Deserves... a distributor who knows if they work the simple system then they will get the support and results they deserve.

Delivers great duplicatable trainings that others can copy... a distributor who coaches the same system they were taught, knowing it will bring results and success.

Doesn't try to control... a distributor who encourages others to come forward and get involved, allowing them to grow, develop and be recognized in their own right.

Draws the circles... a distributor who knows that mere words are not enough and is confident to show the power of Network Marketing through examples using circles and numbers.

Feeds their mind... a distributor who knows that learning is an on-going never-ending process. By constantly reading and listening, they further their own knowledge and can then pass it on to others.

Has a business mentality... a distributor who treats the business like a business, working consistently on it each day. They expect, not hope, to make money and to be successful.

Has a wealth consciousness... a distributor who knows that there is the potential to make a huge amount of money and also sees the need to invest the profits wisely.

Has an attitude of gratitude... a distributor who never fails to be appreciative of the unlimited opportunities they have been given to enjoy the lifestyle of their dreams and for personal growth and development.

Has total belief in Network Marketing... a distributor who has studied the facts versus the myths about Network Marketing and who will never ever let the ill-informed *"dream- stealer"* take away their vision of where they are going. Their belief is passionate, totally unshakable and this distributor will always succeed.

Is confident... a distributor who will attract others to themselves like a magnet. People will always follow confident, strong leaders.

Is on a voicemail system... a distributor who knows the importance of communication and plugs into the voicemail system. They also encourage those in their team to do so the same.

Is on the Internet... a distributor who knows that we are in the 21st century and sees the Internet as a powerful tool for promoting their business, coaching their successline and talking to people globally.

Makes sure that a welcome letter is sent... a distributor who knows the value of keeping in touch with a welcome letter or well-done card. This is very important as it creates a sense of belonging and value.

Never says, *"I know"*... a distributor who knows they will never know it all and who is constantly seeking out more information.

Places new prospects into the process every month... a distributor who knows without doubt, that to sponsor each and every month is the lifeblood of their business.

Plugs in to greatness... a distributor who will advise their successline to attend all the events that will make a difference in their career, encouraging them to be trained by the great leaders.

Prospects daily... a distributor who will talk to people every single day about their opportunity and the benefits it has to offer. *"Two people a day, brings freedom your way."*

Reads, listens to tapes... a distributor who turns their car into a classroom, prioritizing time for reading to further their knowledge and who has a learning attitude.

Refuses to be average... a distributor who knows that average is halfway to the bottom and is for non-achievers. *Going Diamond* is for champions!

Sets goals... a distributor who knows that goal setting is the key to programming their subconscious mind for success.

Shows the potential of the marketing plan... a distributor who excitedly shares the power of the marketing plan with everyone, from prospects to successline.

Uses a duplicatable training system that gets results... a distributor who knows that the fastest and most direct route to the top is to use a simple duplicatable system, which anyone can be coached to do.

Uses the words: *Us-We-Let's...* a distributor who uses the words us, we, let's, together or as a team, realizes that *Going Diamond* is never about *I* or *me*.

Works their business consistently... a distributor who understands the importance of working consistently; they are consistently consistent.

Works smart... a distributor who knows not only the importance of working hard but of working smart.

Writes newsletters... a distributor who knows the importance of keeping in touch with their successline to recognize achievements, share information and to create a sense of group identity, by doing a monthly newsletter. This will be done monthly via a group mail out, email loop or by an ezine on the Internet.

What kind of distributor are you? The choice is yours, as to whether to follow the *"My Way"* to failure or the *"The Diamond Way"* to success.

 Diamond Tip: Choose wisely!

Why People Become Distributors

Over the years of massively recruiting, we have found reasons why people decide to become distributors. There are many different reasons. Here are the top reasons we have found in our experience. This is just a place to start. When you see people with these characteristics, they can become prime candidates for your opportunity. Don't let them pass you by. Ask everyone who you know with these desires. Then follow up, follow up and follow up!

- An opportunity to gain significance.
- An opportunity to get a lifestyle of prosperity and abundance.
- An opportunity to prove that you can be successful.
- A place to personally grow and prosper.
- A place to start over in life.
- Company philosophy.
- Earn income.
- Flexible hours.
- Free training.
- In control of the growth of the successline from the beginning.
- Is dissatisfied with a current job.
- It's a way to become financially successful in a short period of time.
- Love the products.
- Low investment.
- No territories.
- Opportunity for leadership.
- Tax advantages.
- Wants a purpose.
- Wants recognition.
- Wants companionship.
- Wants the challenge.
- Wants to build independence.
- Wants to build self-confidence.
- Wants to do *"my own thing."*

- Wants to earn rewards.
- Wants to feel important.
- Wants to get out of the house.
- Wants to have *"my own money."*
- Wants to have an opportunity to succeed.
- Wants to have fun while making money.
- Wants to improve themselves.
- Wants to make new friends.
- Wants to meet interesting people.
- Wants to be a trainer.
- Wants flexible hours.
- Wants no pressure.
- Wants to be their own boss.
- Wants to develop leadership skills.
- Wants to develop potential.
- Wants to develop public speaking abilities.
- Wants to earn prizes and trips.
- Wants to have an affiliation with others like themselves.
- Wants to have goals to work toward.
- Wants to learn to relate to people better.
- Wants to provide a service and help people.
- Wants to re-enter the workplace.
- Wants to work flexible hours.
- Wants to work part time and have full time earnings. A place to be passionate about life.

If you want the finer things in life, exclusive homes, luxury cars, yachts, private jets, fine art, precious antiques, vintage wines, exotic travel and much more... Go Diamond!

Have the Spirit of the Rhino

Diamonds have tough skin like the rhino. Challenges, disapointments, and change are all part of growing a large business. Diamonds continue to charge forward and are unstoppable just like the rhino.

Use the products and love them.
Share them with other people.
Sponsor others into the business.
Coach them how to do the same.

"The prizes of life are at the end of each journey, not near the beginning; and it is not given to me to know how many steps are necessary in order to reach my goal. Failure I may still encounter at the thousandth step, yet success hides behind the next bend in the road. Never will I know how close it lies unless I turn the corner...
I will persist until I succeed."

–Og Mandino

Diamond Tip: The person who won't be stopped, won't be stopped. Few people ever go for anything in their life, so the road to a golden opportunity is WIDE open for those who choose to *Go Diamond*. The world will stand aside and let the person who knows where they are going, get there. Be like the rhino, charge ahead.

The Challenge

Let others lead small lives,
but not you.
Let others argue over small things,
but not you.
Let others cry over small hurts,
but not you.
Let others leave their future in
someone else's hands,
but not you.

–Jim Rohn

Chapter 2
Who Joins Network Marketing
The Memory Jogger List

Here is a list of people and professions from all walks of life, which will help you think of people to contact to join you. Get this list into the hands of all of your distributors.

Family, friends and acquaintances and anyone you come into contact with or see in a social or leisure environment:

grandparents	parents	parents' friends
brothers	brother's friends	sisters
sister's friends	aunts	uncles
cousins	in-laws	bridesmaids
best man	partner's family	partner's friends
children's friends	children's friends	family
guides or scouts	friends	old school friends
university friends	social friends	sporting friends
keep-fit friends	holiday friends	church members
greetings card list	neighbors	past neighbors

Workplace:

co-workers	past co-workers	partner's co-workers
current boss	past boss	employees
receptionist	maintenance engineer	union officials
sales reps	customers	former employees
former competitors		

Characteristics (some repeats):

tall	short	thin
obese	married	pregnant
separated	engaged	divorced
single parent	widow/widower	immigrant
ethnic	regional accent	foreign accent

beard	moustache	blonde hair
auburn hair	red hair	balding
employee	works nights	self-employed
employer	unemployed	retired
glasses	apartment	condominium
house	farmer	ride a bike
motor bike	nice car	sports car
graduate	keeps-fit	works-out
body-builder	aerobics	swimmer
skier	runner	golfer
dancer	martial arts	angler
trendy	old fashioned	

Occupations:

actuary	accountancy	acupuncture
advertising	aerobics	agriculture
air crew	artist	architecture
armed forces	antiques	aromatherapy
art	author	bakery
banking	bar work	beautician
biologist	boat building	building
butchery	car hire	caretaking
carpentry	carpet fitting	catering
chemist	chiropody	coast guard
construction	consultancy	decorating
delivery	dental	designing
detective	dietician	doctor
dog breeding	domestic cleaning	driving instruction
dry cleaning	education	electrical
electronics	employment	engineering
engraving	entertainment	estate agency
exhibitions	factory	farming
fashion	fire service	furniture
financial	fitness	florist
forestry	furniture	garage
glasses	extrovert	shy
likeable	fun-loving	successful
twin	people person	enthusiastic
young	middle aged	old
gardening	gas station	gemstones
geology	giftware	golfing
government	grocery	gym instruction
hairdressing	healthcare	herbalist

hi-fi
hotel
image consultancy
insulation
investment
joinery
keep fit
kinesiology
laboratory
laundry
leisurewear
mail order
management
massage
nannying
notary
opera
osteopathy
paragliding
personnel
plumbing
printing
quarantine
real estate
recreation
recycling
refuse collection
sales
ski instruction
student
surveying
tax
technology
tourism
undertaking
upholstery
veterinary
wedding
writing
zoo keeping

homeopathy
housewife
immigration
internet
janitorial
journalism
kennels
kitchens
landscaping
law
library
maintenance
marketing
medical
news agent
nursing
optician
packaging
patenting
pharmaceutical
police
quad biking
quarrying
reception
recruitment
reflexology
restaurant
secretarial
social work
supermarket
tailoring
taxi driver
telecommunication
transportation
underwriting
vending
waste disposal
welding
yachting
zoology

hospital
ice cream
insolvency
interpreting
jewelry
karate
kindergarten
knitwear
languages
lecturing
lingerie
make-up
martial arts
meter reading
night club
odd-job
orthodontics
parachuting
pawnbroker
physiotherapy
postal service
quality control
radiography
recording
riding instruction
refrigeration
revenue
security
stock brokering
surgery
take away
teaching
theatre
travel service
university
voluntary
water skiing
window cleaning
yoga

The *Go Diamond* Success Formula

D+S+D=P [Desire + Sacrifice + Discipline= Preparation]

P+S=C [Preparation + Success = Confidence]

MT+P=P [Mental Toughness + Pride = Perseverance]

If you are prepared, have confidence

and persevere, you will be

on your way to Diamond.

Totally, totally, believe in yourself.

It starts today!

Go Diamond!

 Diamond Tip: Ask everyone!

The *Go Diamond* Check Off List for Peak Performers

Distributors who *Go Diamond* take their goals, visions, desires and attitudes seriously. They want to go for greatness. **They will not be denied.** This is just a beginning of what Diamonds learn along their path. Study these carefully and check each one off that you are already doing. Try to discover where you need to concentrate your efforts.

☐ Before expressing an opinion, I make certain to gather every possible fact and I am not afraid to say, *"I don't know."*

☐ From this day forward, by following a few simple steps, or rules, I can alter the course of my life.

☐ I can afford to be confident, for I control my own working hours and the conditions under which I work.

☐ I do not run an organization or home by consensus management, that is not leadership, that is consensus, not the best way or most effective way.

☐ I have closed the door of my mind to past personal mistakes, and look forward to the future with assurance.

☐ I have the desire to work hard, facing and overcoming difficulties.

☐ I think thoughts through without jumping to false conclusions.

☐ I accept people as individuals. All kinds of people and personalities, races and religions are attracted to Network Marketing.

☐ I adapt easily to a customer, a situation, or a challenge.

☐ I always have two pens with me so that I never have to say I don't have a pen or my pen is out of ink.

☐ I always have a yellow legal pad (we call it a Champion pad) or a journal at meetings to catch important ideas.

☐ I always strive to improve, create, change and bring progress to myself and the world.

☐ I am a good listener.

☐ I am a hope coach.

☐ I am a mover in business.

☐ I am a professional in a world of amateurs.

- ☐ I am a professional. Amateurs hope. Professionals work.
- ☐ I am always striving to improve, create, change and bring progress to myself and the world.
- ☐ I am always teaching five people in my organization to reach five new people in their world to join our opportunity.
- ☐ I am an optimist.
- ☐ I am careful what I say to others, once I have reached a big goal. I don't have to prove anything. I don't say: *"She/He is great, just like me."* I am more secure. I say, *"She/He's great!"* Period.
- ☐ I am confident in my abilities to achieve my goals and dreams. I will not be denied a fabulous future.
- ☐ I am considerate of others.
- ☐ I am cooperative.
- ☐ I am curious.
- ☐ I am dissatisfied.
- ☐ I am fortified against occasional, temporary, barriers.
- ☐ I am going down the road to success, wealth, health, happiness, joy, peace of mind.
- ☐ I am going to live the lifestyle I have worked hard to achieve.
- ☐ I am great at delegating and others realize this about me.
- ☐ I am kind and forgiving to myself.
- ☐ I am like Teflon, I let small hurts just slide right off of me.
- ☐ I am more forceful in dealing with negatives from management.
- ☐ I am not average, I am a Champion!
- ☐ I am not bored with my job.
- ☐ I am part of the solution, not the challenge.
- ☐ I am polished. Think of silver that is tarnished, it takes a while to polish it, but isn't silver beautiful when it shines?
- ☐ I anticipate success.
- ☐ I arrive at my customers or hostess with a program or presentation already worked out; one that often needed very little adjustment to fit the customer's needs.
- ☐ I ask myself, *"If I knew I couldn't lose, what would I shoot for?"* There is *No Limit.*
- ☐ I believe in a higher power, and angels have directed me.
- ☐ I believe in myself—I believe in others and keep that in mind.
- ☐ I believe that I can achieve by learning everything about the business.
- ☐ I call twenty people a day and ask for referrals.
- ☐ I can forgive those who have hurt me. The energy it takes to stay hurt or angry can be very detrimental to my future personal growth.
- ☐ I check in with my Upline frequently.
- ☐ I close the door of my mind to past personal mistakes, and look forward to the future with assurance.

- ❑ I develop an effective action plan and stick to it.
- ❑ I do much more than is expected of me and do not expect extra compensation.
- ❑ I do not run an organization or home by consensus management, that is not leadership, that is consensus, not the best way or most effective way.
- ❑ I do not seek personal praise, but am quick to give praise and encouragement to others.
- ❑ I do what I can do to resolve hurts that are painful to me.
- ❑ I don't and won't follow the herd.
- ❑ I don't avoid opportunity.
- ❑ I don't believe in luck. I believe in focusing on goals and going to work on myself to be the best I can be.
- ❑ I don't divide others into *"winners"* and *"losers"*.
- ❑ I don't hide behind busy work.
- ❑ I don't live a boxed life.
- ❑ I don't stroll to a goal.
- ❑ I don't talk only about my own situations and victories. I listen carefully to cheer on others when they are victorious.
- ❑ I don't engage in superstitious thoughts. When something bad happens, I don't assume that more bad things are likely to follow. I am an optimist.
- ❑ I don't restrict my thinking by establishing rigid patterns.
- ❑ I don't waste time in unproductive thoughts.
- ❑ I dream big. My dreams are going to see me through.
- ❑ I envision myself as a leader—even when I walk into a grocery store, I say to myself—*"I am a Leader!"*
- ❑ I establish clear priorities.
- ❑ I expect miracles, I am not surprised at them.
- ❑ I feed my engines with fuel from books, tapes, seminars, and people with experiences, wisdom, rest, relaxation and recreation.
- ❑ If I am correct and you don't bother to heed my words, won't you be sorry?
- ❑ If I can't do anything about a negative situation, I don't worry or fret about it, I move on.
- ❑ If I have the need to seek something that I do not have, to improve my life, I will seek it until I find it.
- ❑ I find out all I can about a prospective customer before I even call for an appointment.
- ❑ I find solutions.
- ❑ I find success is rewarding.
- ❑ I find that being average is disgusting.

☐ I focus my thoughts on the task at hand.

☐ I give myself a check up from the neck up from time to time.

☐ I have a constant list with many names on it—my top customers from last year to recontact.

☐ I have a fearless nature.

☐ I have a gratitude attitude.

☐ I have a positive attitude everyday.

☐ I have an important message for others to hear.

☐ I have chairpersons for everything you can think of. For meetings, for ideas, for refreshments, for newsletter ideas, etc.

☐ I have daily motivation to do the right thing.

☐ I have developed a winning attitude. Champions want to win, winning is everything to a true champion.

☐ I have developed an effective action plan and stick to it.

☐ I have developed an effective emotional plan of how I will react when disappointed. I will not stew, I will do.

☐ I have eliminated the words *"I know"* from my vocabulary.

☐ I have flexibility.

☐ I have great self-reliance and self-confidence.

☐ I have greeters at meetings.

☐ I have integrity.

☐ I have sufficient motivation to come up with a new idea if my old one is turned down.

☐ I have the ability to accept difficulties without complaints.

☐ I have the ability to roll with the punches.

☐ I have the ability to strive and achieve despite great odds.

☐ I have the need to seek something that I do not have, to improve my life.

☐ I have the only one basic requirement that is necessary to produce this *"self-miracle,"* called desire.

☐ I have the willingness to go, to perform, to pursue an objective with all my heart and soul.

☐ I help others succeed.

☐ I hug my family more.

☐ I keep in mind that the givers in life of time and energy make more money than the givers of material items.

☐ I keep motivated to work hard every day.

☐ I know and concentrate on the fact that the great successlines have not yet been built and I will help others build bigger and better successlines than I did.

☐ I make decisions.

☐ I make it my business to mentally renew myself for every prospect.

☐ I memorize quotes until they become part of me. I will not allow myself to be affected by things out of control so that I despair of this precious life. I won't make that terrible mistake.

- [ ] I never allow anyone to push my kill switch.
- [ ] I never cut corners.
- [ ] I never dump down during a challenging time; I always dump up to the upline.
- [ ] I never neglect little things (even though there is a book that says Don't Sweat the Small Stuff).
- [ ] I never take sides until I have heard both sides.
- [ ] I never tell a child his/her dreams are unlikely or outlandish. Few things are more humiliating, and what a tragedy it would be if he/she believed me.
- [ ] I only judge a person's circumstances well enough to know just what to say.
- [ ] I plan to work and work my plan.
- [ ] I provide better attitude. No stinkin' thinking with me.
- [ ] I put behind me past hurts.
- [ ] I realize no excuses are acceptable. None.
- [ ] I realize that I am subject to errors, but I am determined to profit by my own learning experiences.
- [ ] I realize that if I have done what I can do then really, it's the other person's challenge and I can't take on other people's challenges.
- [ ] I realize that many times people don't realize they have hurt me so deeply and it serves no purpose to harbor bitter feelings, life is too short, I get over it and move on with my life, I can't change what happened five minutes ago.
- [ ] I realize that temporary reversals do happen, even when there may be no apparent cause.
- [ ] I refuse to let my mind drift to unpleasant events of the past, waste of time, water under the bridge.
- [ ] I remember FAYC= forget about yourself completely.
- [ ] I resolve to have a New Years Resolution to be more forgiving.
- [ ] I see each day as a series of new adventures.
- [ ] I seek out winners, and run away from negative people.
- [ ] I tell the truth.
- [ ] I think constructively which saves me from wasting time and suffering psychological pain.
- [ ] I think constructively. I know that there is no charge for thinking.
- [ ] I think in ways that facilitate effective action.
- [ ] I treat each new presentation as a distinct challenge.
- [ ] It's not where I am that is important. It's where I am going.
- [ ] It's not what I have in my life, but whom I have in my life.

- ☐ I turn off the TV set.
- ☐ I understand that being average puts me, as close to the bottom of the best and at the top of the worst, I will not hang out with the average people.
- ☐ I understand that faith is a lot like love- it can't be forced. I must give others faith that they can succeed.
- ☐ I use phrases that I am hearing from Champions—I choose to use their words.
- ☐ I value my most precious treasure, my self-respect.
- ☐ I visualize myself with some of my team on the incentive trip.
- ☐ I welcome challenges with optimism.
- ☐ I will attend more seminars, read more books, listen to more tapes, and will continue to feed my mind.
- ☐ I will continue to persist until I succeed.
- ☐ I will direct my organization towards personal growth and development starting with my own program of being a student.
- ☐ I will focus my thoughts on the task at hand.
- ☐ I will get and stay high on life.
- ☐ I will get better computer skills.
- ☐ I will give out at least 25-50 business cards per week.
- ☐ I will never give up or shut up about success and going for greatness.
- ☐ I will not be denied the lifestyle.
- ☐ I will not fail to plan. Failures don't plan to fail. . . they just fail to plan.
- ☐ I will not make excuses that I am in an area where no one wants to recruit with me, I will take responsibility that I need to work on my presentation skills, my appearance, my voice, my clothes until I find the key for my future success in mastering recruiting.
- ☐ I will put away clutter.
- ☐ I will quit hiding behind busy work.
- ☐ I will respond quickly.
- ☐ I will sail away from the safe harbor.
- ☐ I will save 10% of every check no matter how many bills I have to pay.
- ☐ I will set aside the same two hours a day to work.
- ☐ I will stay *Fired Up!* even when others around me are not. I will lead by example.
- ☐ I will stay motivated, feeling that *"I'm good enough and I am really making a difference."*
- ☐ I will stop avoiding opportunity.
- ☐ I will take a moment to be thankful that I am alive.
- ☐ I will take at least 10-15 minutes a day to read a motivational book.
- ☐ I will take time to smile.
- ☐ I will think before I react.

- [ ] I work fast; work smart.
- [ ] Lead me, follow me or get out of my way.
- [ ] My job is to move more products and get more people.
- [ ] One of the most difficult lessons I have learned is how to see and appreciate the beauty right here on earth. I will take care of the planet.
- [ ] Success, joy, wealth, love, and fulfillment, are all available to me now.
- [ ] The person who says it can't be done is often interrupted by the person who is doing it.
- [ ] There is always someone who wants to be the best.
- [ ] There is no letter *"I"* in the word *"team."*
- [ ] These aspirations are powered by still another source for strength and action, all these are mileposts on the road to success.
- [ ] When I am faced with a difficulty, I find a way to look at the positive side of life.
- [ ] When I have to choose between what is right and what is advantageous, I always choose to do what's right.
- [ ] When I need a quote I don't get credit for reading it, I don't get credit for underlining it. I only get the credit if I take it and use it.
- [ ] When I speak of others, I make every effort to avoid emphasizing their faults, regardless of how obvious these failings must be.

"Would you tell me, please, which way I ought to go from here?"

"That depends a good deal on where you want to get to," said the Cat.

"I don't much care where," said Alice.

"Then it doesn't matter which way you go," said the Cat.

(From Alice in Wonderland)

STP =

See the people
Serve the people
Save the people
Seek total prosperity
Sponsor the persistent

And *whatever you do*,
sponsor, train and
prospect and teach
others to do the same!

Go Diamond!

8 Steps To Give You Time To Work Your Business Smarter

We wake up in the morning. We don't have a boss. We have choices and when *Going Diamond*, we must be self-motivated. No one is there to cheer us on or encourage us first thing in the morning. We can exercise, shower, then get dressed. Next, we make breakfast for the children and get them off to school. If we have a pet, we take the pet outside for a walk. We can read a book, listen to a tape, or start our list of what we want to accomplish for the day. We make and take telephone calls, plan meetings, our successline begins to grow, we are fired up and ready to follow up on our leads and prospect even more. We have a goal to *Go Diamond*, and even though we don't want it to be so long, our to-do list is up to six pages long.

Later, on we pick up our children from school, or take them to lessons or watch them at soccer practice, or help them with their homework, do some chores, and begin making dinner. When the family is finished eating, there are dishes to be washed, and perhaps clothes to be put in the wash or clothes that need to be folded and put away.

Then, maybe we do some ironing, check our e-mail and begin getting the kids ready for bed. Before we know it, it's time for bed and just to get to tomorrow, which is basically an exact duplicate of today. And we begin to think there is just no time to fit in building a home based business much less *Going Diamond!*

Whew! It's only a matter of time before we are completely burnt out and begin to think of giving up—especially if we feel the described above pales in comparison to our schedule!

It's time to slow down, and gain control of your life again. Here are eight simple ways to calm down, and to fit your life into your vision of *Going Diamond*:

1. Make a list of the truly important things to be done: Get a spiral notebook, or a sheet of paper, and make a numbered list, one through ten. Next, list the things in your life that are most important to you. Next, take some quiet time and ask yourself if the way you currently spend your time, matches your list of important things. You'll then have a better idea of what things you need to spend more time on. As you *Go Diamond*, know that you will have to-do lists more and more. Keep them all where you can get to them hourly. Cross off what you are achieving and go to work on the next item on your list.

2. Determine what your habits are: For the next two weeks, write down everything you do in your spiral notebook and the amount of time you spend doing it. At the end of the two week period, analyze your log, and determine what areas of your life need to be streamlined. Example challenged areas are: spending the majority of your time at your computer, or doing four hours worth of chores each day. When you are *Going Diamond*, you have to learn to say *"No"* to many distractions. Focus on building your business to the Diamond level. There is plenty of time to do charity work in the future.

3. Use your time wisely, don't waste it: During your time in the car, listen to a motivational tape or CD or some music to lift your spirit and get you in a productive mood. Do more than one thing at a time. Put the clothes in the wash, turn on the dishwasher, put catalogs under the seat of your car, make phone calls on your cell phone while you are folding clothes, and just combine whatever you can to do more than one thing at a time. Hurry, you can't stroll to a goal. Work smarter. As you *Go Diamond*, you will work very hard and feel like you have no time to yourself. When you get to Diamond, or before while you are on your way, you will be able to afford support people to help you grow your business even faster. You can get a housekeeper, a bookkeeper, a gardener, a pool person to keep your pool clean, someone to wax your fancy car and keep it gassed up, the lifestyle is amazing.

4. Get a simple wardrobe: Stop, or reduce, buying dry clean only clothes, so you're not constantly running back and forth to the dry cleaners. Wash clothes regularly, so they don't build up. Make sure you have comfortable and clean shoes when you exit your home. If you can get two or three wearings out of something before you wash it, you'll reduce your laundry time. Many times the clothes you're wearing today will still be clean tomorrow. Most people only wear 20% of the clothes they have. The rest just sit in closets and drawers. Throw out the clothes you no longer enjoy wearing and those that don't fit you or are out of style. As you *Go Diamond*, you will be able to wear the latest fashions and enjoy shopping not on a budget.

5. Set aside family time: Are you forever driving the children all over town for their after-school activities? You might decree that each child is only allowed one extracurricular activity at a time. Make sure that you spend quality family time, not quantity. Your children do not need you 24/7/365. Most parents need their children's time more than the children need the parents' time. Do not make your family your excuse why you cannot *Go Diamond*, make them your **reason** that you **DO** *Go Diamond!* If you want your children to get involved in lots of activities, work out a drop off and pick up schedule with your spouse, a relative, a friend or a neighbor. Consider starting a car pool club. You drop off and pick up the children on Mondays, rotate with another parent on Tuesdays, etc. As you *Go Diamond*, visualize taking your family on fantastic vacations and building amazing memories.

6. Streamline your office: Are you always working late in your office? Can you delegate more, or can you use your computer to speed up the time it takes to complete a regular task? Can you hire an assistant? If you have your own business already, is it possible to outsource some of your work? If you're the *"only person that can do the job right,"* your schedule is always going to be full. Learn to delegate. As you streamline your office, you will have more time to work on prospecting, following up and recruiting and selling. As you *Go Diamond*, you will be able to afford faster computers, laptops to take on trips to lighten your work when you get back home, palm pilots or handheld computers, and gadgets that will help you do your business faster.

7. Throw out the clutter: When you begin to declutter your home and your office, you'll realize how much time it can save you to live and work in an organized environment. When your surroundings are decluttered, your mind has a chance to relax, and focus. Get rid of clutter. Get a huge plastic bag and start throwing out all the pieces of paper in piles that have been sitting there for months. Weed out old and outdated paperwork. Donate things you no longer use. Give items you do use a permanent place that you will put them every time so that they are there when you need them. Get rid of old e-mails that have been sitting on your computer for months. Dump your delete box out often. Lighten up your wardrobe, your pantry, your basement and your attic—you'll be amazed at what you can actually live without, and what you WON'T miss. You'll spend less time looking for things, fretting over feelings of chaos, and more time enjoying your life and you will get much more accomplished. As you lighten your load, remember that as you *Go Diamond*, you can throw out the old and replace it with new.

56

8. **Manage your kitchen:** Cooking dinner? Make enough for two nights. It rarely takes additional time to double a meal, but it saves tons of time if you just have to heat up some of those leftovers later in the week, rather than cooking an entirely new meal. You can even make enough for two meals and freeze a portion for next week. If you do this each night for one whole week, you will have seven ready-meals for the entire next week. Just defrost, heat and eat. Cook meals that don't take hours of preparation. While it's OK to do this once in awhile for special occasions, regular daily meals should not involve more than twenty minutes of preparation. Get good kitchen supplies that making cooking fun. Get some great fast recipes from distributors in the cooking Network Marketing companies. As you *Go Diamond*, you will be able to afford a Chef and dine at fabulous restaurants and have gourmet dinners all over the world. Keep the big picture in mind.

Perhaps nothing else in life has such strong ability to capture one's eyes and attention like a Diamond.

 Diamond Tip: Touch your business every day.

Chapter 3
Creating Affluence

Once upon a time in a faraway land…a young man went to the forest and said to his spiritual master,

"I want to have unlimited wealth and with that unlimited wealth, I want to help and heal the world. Will you please tell me the secret to creating affluence?"

And the spiritual master replied,

"There are two Goddesses that reside in the heart of every human being. Everybody is deeply in love with these supreme beings. But there is a certain secret that you need to know, and I will tell you what it is."

"Although you love both Goddesses, you must pay more attention to one of them. One is the Goddess of Knowledge, and her name is Sarasvati. Pursue her, love her, and give her your attention. The other Goddess, whose name is Lakshmi, is the Goddess of Wealth. When you pay more attention to Sarasvati, Lakshmi will become extremely jealous and pay more attention to you. The more you seek the the Goddess of Knowledge the more the Goddess of Wealth will seek you. She will follow you wherever you go and never leave you. And the wealth you desire will be yours forever."

**There is power in knowledge, desire, and spirit.
And this power within you is the key to *creating affluence*.**

 Diamond Tip: Feed your mind. Before financial freedom can take place there first must be personal growth and development.

Become a Master Prospector

Prospecting and follow up is the life-blood of the business. *"Where do I get my prospects?"* is a common question asked by distributors. Here are some powerful tips to help you be a master prospector and train others to be one too:

The *"Warm Market"* Contact List:

Using a warm market contact list is a core skill and provides one of the most powerful and effective methods of prospecting. It is based on the simple exercise of preparing a comprehensive list of people we already know, which we call *"warm market"* or *"contact"* list. It's a gold mine! Who better to share a new business with, than people you already know? Very often in a new distributor's early days and before they really have *"got to grips"* with the need for a comprehensive list, they will claim that, *"I don't know anyone."* It's very common for new distributors to say this and often suggests that they haven't yet given it much thought or that they are prejudging people they know and leaving them off their list. Train new distributors just how simple it is to expand a warm market list and to have fun doing it. Here are some fabulous tips to help you do just that!

1. **Prepare a *"Who do I know?"* list of at least 100 names**. If there are only thirty names on a list, then working on the average that one in ten people they talk to will join the business, there is little chance to sponsor more than three or four people. If there are 100 or more on the list and it's constantly being added to, this gives a good start and takes away the worry of running out of prospects.

2. **Expand the list, by playing *"the name game"* or word association, on each name**. For example, if Jeff Bell is listed, suggest that underneath the name, add other names that are linked by word association. Here is an example of the questions to ask to do this: *"Do you know anyone else called Jeff? Do you know anyone else with the last name Bell? What does Jeff do for a living and do you know anyone else with the same occupation? Where does he live and who else do you know who lives there? Is he married, what*

is his wife's name and who else do you know with that name? Do they have children? Where do they go to school? Who else do you know with children at that school? What hobbies does Jeff have and do you know anyone else with similar hobbies? What car does he drive?" It really is simple to spark off a train of thought that will in turn lead to other names. Many times, it's not uncommon to add another ten or twenty names for each existing name on the list. It's a fun and productive way to expand the list.

3. **Use the Memory Jogger List in Chapter 2 as a way of coming up with new names**. This gets distributors really thinking about people they may know from all walks of life.

4. **Prepare a full list.** Never prejudge anyone. This is not a business of prejudging other people's needs. Simply offer people a life-changing opportunity and give prospects the right to decide for themselves if they want to get involved. Many successful distributors have walked past thousands of pounds or dollars worth of monthly income, simply because they prejudged people they knew and in turn denied them the opportunity to join them and to be hugely successful. Very often, they decided not to ask, someone else did and they lost a possible future leader.

Referrals From Your *"Who Do You Know"* List:

There will be people who say, *"No"* to your opportunity. Sadly these people will just not be able to see what you see and that's okay. Train how to ask for referrals. Almost everyone knows someone for whom their opportunity would be just great. Usually when a distributor has made the call to a prospect and they have said that it's not for them, they don't find out whether that means *"no, not ever,"* as against *"no, not now,"* or **think of asking for referrals**. Example script: *"Well, I'm really sorry, John, that the opportunity isn't for you right now. I had you down, as one of the top-ten people I would most like to work with. However, things change, so let's keep-in-touch. In the meantime, I'm looking for just a few key people who are like you, with good attitudes and who want to make a six-figure income. Do you know anyone like that and may I contact them?"* Most times, they will respond that they cannot think of anyone and that is an understandable reaction to a question asked *"out of the blue,"* next tell them that you would appreciate their help and will give them a quick call within 24 hours, to see if they have thought of someone. Then tell them that as a *"thank you"* for their help, you will be sending them a complimentary product. If you don't ask, you will never get. People will want to help you, if you learn to ask in the right way.

Contact Marketing:

We all come into contact every day with people we don't know but with whom we can communicate. This could be in a store, paying for goods; in a restaurant and ordering from the server; in a work environment and coming into contact with new people; or simply going out bowling with the family, or to the cinema or swimming. Contact Marketing is also about being able to *"exit your home and prospect hunt."*

Be prepared. *"Dress for success,"* look very smart, people buy distributors first and the message second. Have business cards, a small note pad or palm-top, a nice pen and your company recruiting information in the form of leaflets, videos, and/or recruiting brochures with you. Be mentally prepared to do business, with a clear objective as to how long you will stay in town, probably an hour or so, how many new leads you are going to get and where you are going to do it.

You are now ready to look for your first prospect:

Even with preparation in place, new distributors find stopping a stranger in the street, a fearful thing to do. One of the easiest ways to engage in conversation is to stop someone and ask for their help. This gives you reason to talk to them and with it, the opportunity to talk about your business. Example, *"Excuse me, can you tell me where the library is?"* or, *"Excuse me, can you help me? I'm looking for the coffee shop above the book shop."* When the person responds, you can thank them for their help, then say, *"I'm in town on business and meeting up with some colleagues; we're expanding our business here and are recruiting at the moment. I know this is an unusual approach but would you be open to some free information on what we do?"* Most people will ask, *"What is it?"* to which you reply, *"I can't talk now as I am running late for my meeting but I do have some information I can give you to look at; all I ask is that I can have your name and number, so I can give you a phone call to see what you think of it. Is that good for you?"* Most times, they will agree to take your information and be happy to accept a follow-up call; simply exchange details, thank them for their time and confirm you will call them within 48 hours to have a chat. Make the point that if they like what they see, you will take it to the next step and if not, you won't. Keep it light and friendly and don't go into masses of detail. It is simple, inexpensive, duplicatable, great fun and effective. It will require some practice. Prospect regularly and once you are happy with this prospecting approach you will find that it's such a simple way to get even **more prospects**.

Websites are a popular way to promote business and are a simple way to direct contacts to your site. Have nice business cards made giving your phone number, mobile, fax, voicemail, email and especially your website address. On the back of the card, have a simple recruiting message to act as a reminder to the prospect, encouraging them to look at the web address. A good contact marketing card may look like this:

John Curtis
Senior Partner
QLS Group

Telephone: +44 (0)1600 740
Mobile: +44 (0)7710 832 004
Voicemail: +44 (0)1327 659 128
Email:john@glsgroup.com
Web:www.nolimitspeople.com

On the back of the card, a simple message to remind your prospect why they have your card:

Time for a change?
· What if your life changed, because you had the money and
  freedom to change it, to anything you wanted it to be?
· You don't have to put up with being under valued, over stressed,
  bored, job insecurity or having no time or future.
· There is a better way and it will cost you nothing to find out how
  to add extra thousands per month to your income, without
  compromising your current career…and you may just end up
  having the time of your life!
Call us today or visit our website
www.nolimitspeople.com

These cards are fantastic for *"breaking the ice"* when talking to someone you have just met and don't know. Here are some great ideas on how to give these cards out:

• You have just enjoyed a good meal and the person serving you was really helpful, then when you go to pay your check, make sure you compliment them for their service and give out a card. Example, *"Thanks for the great service you've given me. With your attitude and great customer care, you would be fantastic in my business. Here's my card – visit my web site or call me and I will send you a free information packet; better still, let me jot down your number and I will give you a call."*

• You go to a store to buy something and have someone help you find what you need. Example, *"Thanks for your help. I really appreciate it. How long have you been working here? Well, I run my own very successful business and I'm always looking for people like you, with good people skills. Here's my card; if you want to find out more, visit my web site or give me a call and I will send you some free information; better still, let me jot down your number and I will give you a call later when it's more convenient to talk. Thanks again for your help."*

• You are in a coffee shop, bar, or café, and strike up a conversation with someone, during the course of which they ask what you do. Example: *"Well, I run my own very successful business, under the umbrella of a major international company. I'm recruiting right now and looking for some ambitious people, keen to make large incomes and help others do the same. Here's my card. Give me a call or visit the web site and let's see if there is something there for you."*

Many people work their business part-time around an existing job or career; during their lunch breaks, they may have need to *"walk into town"* to get some lunch. A great opportunity now presents itself to give out cards to other people like them, who may also be working in the same sort of environment, and who may be looking for a second income or for a complete change. The very thought of working in the same office for the next ten years could fill them with dread! Lots of people are looking for a better way to earn a living and you have the solution. Simply engage them in a conversation that will lead to a card being given out. When waiting in a queue (line), waiting to pay for your lunch, it's simple to engage in conversation. Example: *"These lines never get any better, do they?"* or, *"Well, it won't be long before I don't have to line up for lunch here anymore."* They may ask why that is, to which you reply, *"I have a business which I have been working part-time around my current job and it's become so successful, I will soon be leaving the day-job. Come to think of it, you might be interested in looking at what I do. Here is my card, give me a call and we can talk further or you can visit my web site."* It's easy to just engage in chitchat; it breaks the ice and allows you to talk further or to give them your card and ask them to call you.

Contact marketing is being prepared to talk to everyone you meet about your opportunity. Have some business cards to portray a professional image. Never miss an opportunity to sponsor someone like you. In today's economic times, everyone wants and needs security for themselves and their family - they are just waiting to be asked and then shown a better way, or a new way to achieve their dreams.

Diamond Tip: Make sure you ask everyone to join you!
Share your opportunity every chance you get!
Two new friends a day brings freedom my way!

Help distributors to become comfortable with the words to use and share stories with them about people sponsored into the organization by using this method.

Prospecting by Using Flyers and Posters:

Flyers are good to hand out to people in the street, at shows, exhibitions, concerts, the subway or railway station; anywhere where there are large gatherings of people. It's really fun to do. Have distributors work in couples or as a team and in about one hour, they can each quite easily give out 200 plus flyers. Some people will refuse to take them, but don't take it personally; just give those people a big smile and hand out the flyer to the next person who comes along. When handing out flyers, it is important to look your best, since *"people buy people first"* and they will take the message on the flyer more seriously, if the distributor handing it to them looks successful. Never give out flyers while dressed in jeans and a T-shirt; it won't work. Dress to impress.

When a team is going out to work together, arrange to meet at a local coffee shop. Decide who will be working with whom. Decide on how many flyers to give out and make a plan not to stop until they are all gone. Then plan what time to meet back at the coffee shop, in order to have a quick debrief, share success stories, have some fun and agree when to meet and do it again. Sometimes when flyers are handed out, people will come back and ask what is it all about. Be ready and carry a pocket-size notebook or palm-top, to be ready to take details of how to contact the new person they have met. Ask them their name, followed by a brief explanation, in a couple of minutes, of what they are doing. Example: *"Thanks. My name is Joe; what's yours?"* [they respond] *"Dave, I am working in this area with a very successful company and today we are giving out some information, encouraging people like you to find out more. I know it's an unusual approach but we find it to be very effective. We are looking for open-minded, ambitious individuals or couples, who want to make an extra 500 to 1,500 a month part-time, 5,000 to 10,000 or more a month full-time. Would you like to find out more, without obligation? I can give you a free audio or video tape; or recruiting brochure, which would you prefer?"*

Example flyers:

Excuse the unusual approach but would you be
interested in an **amazing second income**
We are looking for ambitious individuals and couples
who want to earn
1,000 to 5,000 or more per month
full-time or part- time, without it affecting
your current job or business
Call +44 (0)1600 740 146
www.jayneleach.com

**Whatever your profession, could you benefit from
a secure second income?**

Here's the simplest business opportunity we have
ever encountered!

**Part-time 500 to 1,500 per month
Full-time 5,000 to 10,000 or more**

No experience necessary, as full training and
support program available.

Interested?
**Call +44 (0)1600 740 146 today for a free information pack
or visit www.nolimitspeople.com**

Go into the local town or community and put flyers onto store windows, on notice boards, in the library, health club, post office, supermarket or anywhere you can think. It's a simple and inexpensive way of marketing yourself and your message. The list of where you can put them is endless; it's all about being creative and proactive. There only needs to be one good reply from a card or flyer, resulting in a person joining and subsequently reaching a key position on the compensation plan, and its all been worthwhile. You just never know who is looking. Here are some examples for cards and small posters for shop windows or for putting out into your community. Be as creative as you want. Create a flyer, promoting your products, and opportunity. Here is another example:

Advertising In Newspapers And Magazines:

This is one area of prospecting that we don't encourage in the early days of a new distributor joining a team. It can be expensive and there are no guarantees that it will work. To be successful, it requires the choice of the right publication and a message strong enough to attract attention and to then prompt the reader to respond, not just think about responding. Many good communication skills and patience are required to deal with the response. Advertising can work well for a more experienced person, but the challenge with running adverts is that it is not duplicatable. The further away from warm marketing and contact marketing you go, the less likely you are to duplicate yourself to the masses. That can create challenges with team members because if they all suddenly go out and put the same or a similar advert into the same local paper, let's say seven or eight people advertising from the same company, it will give out a confusing message to potential prospects and it may cause friction between team members as they argue over who prospects belongs to. What if none of them get a response? It can cause great negativity and dampen the spirits of the team. We are not saying it doesn't work; we are suggesting that it is inappropriate to teach and coach new team members.

T-shirts, Sweatshirts and Button Badges:

Be creative and have fun in your marketing. Have some T-shirts and sweatshirts made up with your team logo and a simple message promoting your business. Example: *"Recruiting now, ask for your free info,"* or *"Need more money? Want more fun? Want new friends? Ask me about my business,"* or *"Want a second income of 500 to 1,500 a month? Ask me how!"* Be as creative as you want. Wear this clothing to the gym, a great place for people to read your message; or go out in groups with your team and do some contact marketing, wearing them. If you are doing a show or an exhibition, wear them there. Have some small button badges made up with simple messages, such as:

Want to know a secret? Ask me!

What is your future? Ask me!

Grow old gratefully. Ask me how!

Ask me what I play with!

Network Marketing is the same as any other form of marketing in that the essential first step is to attract attention. All of the above ideas are great attention grabbers and are proven to work. All you are looking for is ways to get people interested in your message and to talk to you out of curiosity.

The *"Chicken List:"*

Ah, the famous *"chicken list;"* we all have one and at some time or another, we have been *"almost scared to death"* to talk to these people. What is it? Well, if someone has done their *"Who Do You Know?"* contact list including on it absolutely everyone they know, without exception, they will have people on that list who they perceive to be better than themselves. It might be because they are more successful, ambitious, or because they have prejudged them to be too busy, wealthier or just to have a high standard of life, mixing with people they don't mix with. All too often, they look at these people and say to themselves, *"I couldn't possibly talk to them; they are far too successful, wealthy, and higher up in the social structure"* or some other negative self talk. These are the contacts that we are just too *"chicken"* to call.

The good news is that these will be some of the very best prospects, because they may already have an amazing lifestyle but the price they pay for it, may be way too high. Perhaps they are massively successful but have to work 70 -80 hours a week and in doing so, are missing out on the most precious and valuable element of their lives, something they can never get back....time. Or missing out on their children growing up, long holidays or simply just having the time to watch a movie or play some football. These prospects are used to making a lot of money but you have what they desperately want and need, freedom and the ability to have the high standard of living and income, without the 70-80 hours a week to get it. Also, keep in mind that every eagle knows a sparrow. They might **know someone who would be interested.** Who would you be sick to find out joined someone else in your successline because you were scared to offer them the opportunity?

This is an exciting world. It is jam-packed with opportunity.
Great moments await you around every corner.

 Diamond Tip: Attach more fear to not contacting everyone you know than to contacting everyone you know.

The Path to *Diamond:*
One + One = *Go Diamond!*

It all starts with making a decision to be unstoppable and to get to the top position of your compensation plan. You start by sponsoring one person and selling product, then teaching that person to do the same.

Train new distributors to:
•go to the top of the compensation plan.
•keep catalogs with them at all times.
•sell products at least once a week. You must sell to get paid.
•sponsor at least one new person into your personal team per month who sells product and sponsors at least one new person a month…who sells product and sponsors one person a month.
•talk to at least one person every day about the opportunity.
•talk to at least one person every day about the products.
•sell product each week, the goal is to have 4 home parties a month OR sell 500 dollars or pounds.
•not wait on the upline or anyone to motivate them, just get out there and do it! Hurry and cash in on the fun and the rewards.
•sponsor at least one new person per month….you cannot get to the top without sponsoring people. You must not manage your team and fail to recruit personally, that is not Diamond behavior. Lead the field by recruiting every month. Do not let the month end without having a recruit.
•train, train, train each new person to do the same.
•sell, sponsor, train and teach others to do the same.
•tell others how…..show them how…..and watch them do it.

Thousands of home parties happen every single week. Parties, demos, shows and launches are hot.

These are the cornerstone for *Going Diamond.* The fundamentals. Do them over and over again. When you do this on a consistent basis for a one-year period of time, you are not going to believe your results.

Here are results that could happen if you are consistently building a business. The results speak for themselves. Here is an example with the assumption that each distributor, including you will:
•Sell a minimum of $50 wholesale per week, and
•Sponsor just one person per month, and train that person to do the same.

Month	Distributors	Sales
1 + 1=	2	$ 400
2	4	600
3	8	1,600
4	16	3,200
5	32	6,400
6	64	12,800
7	128	25,600
8	256	51,200
9	512	102,400
10	1024	204,800
11	2048	409,600
12	4096	$818,200

OK, now this is the math.... you decide when you are ready to start sponsoring one person per week or you can decide you are comfortable where you are in life and don't want the lifestyle that is waiting for you on a silver platter.... **your choice.**

To do this, be consistent in your one per month before you make the commitment to go beyond that point.

At your trainings, do an opening to (parties, demos, shows, launches), have everyone take notes and then have EVERY new distributor get up in front of you and do their opening. Train people to do their own Grand Openings. Train them to have confidence that they could do their own first events. Train lots of distributors at the same time, let them practice in front of each other and they will train each other!

> Your range of available choices in life,
> right this very moment is limitless.

 Diamond Tip: Train distributors to build *their own* businesses.

There are just 3 types of distributors:

> # The doers
> # The onlookers
> # The uninterested

The doers make things happen.
The onlookers are the many who watch things happen and make excuses for why they are not growing their businesses.
The uninterested are the largest group who have no idea what is happening and frankly don't care how many times you call them, they are going to stay uninterested.

YOU, the Doer, the future Diamond, the distributor taking action, are the one who does not make excuses, you navigate around whatever the obstacles are, you take risks, and you will not be denied. You will *Go Diamond* once you set your sights on Diamond, and the income and lifestyle being a Diamond will provide you.

Diamonds play a critical role in our industry.

Diamonds take ideas and turn them into realities. Diamonds are the ones who get the entire successline moving. If you have a stagnant upline, just get busy and build an organization. Become the leader; your upline could come out of the mothballs and rise up as a leader as well.

Diamonds achieve what others only dream of.

Going Diamond is just a numbers business. It's all mathematical. We are in the business of getting to the top of the compensation plan. *Go Diamond!*

Have a wealth consciousness. Think abundant and prosperous thoughts. Use your affirmations and all of the gems in this book. Be a peak performer, use The Proven Way, *The Go Diamond System* and pay attention to the details shared in this book. Get your personal growth and development program of CANEI, **C**onstant **A**nd **N**ever **E**nding **I**mprovement started immediately. Readers are leaders and leaders are readers. Study affluence, use tons of visuals in your business, start your own sizzle sessions, see the people and be willing to try new ideas! *Fire Up!* There are truly *No Limits* on where you can take yourself. *Go Diamond!*

The Ambassador Club

Here's a great idea you can give to a person who might become a potential Host/Hostess...explain that it's a challenge.

Call it, **The Ambassador Club.**

Ask people who are not interested in having a party, demo, show or launch, if they would like to be part of your **Ambassador Club.**

This is what they will commit to doing: TEN OF ONE of a KIND Opportunity.

This is the reward for meeting the challenge: Free products!

Note: You will want to make sure that this is someone you can trust to give you the orders and the money they collect.

Here is how it works: Choose 5 - 6 different items that are in the $20-$35 price range. Ask a potential host/hostess to select one item, take it with him/her, and to sell 10 of that item **within the next week.**

Give the person several catalogs, *JUST IN CASE* their friends don't want the item being shown, they can still offer them the catalog. Don't put any pressure on the host/hostess to take other orders, but if they do, they will make 10% of whatever they sell towards the purchase of more products forever. Make sure that your name and address and phone number and email address are on all the catalogs.

Tell the host/hostess that if *they get orders from 10 different people that makes them part of your* **"Ambassador Program."**

Set a date approximately one week later to meet with the host/hostess to get your item back and collect the orders. This is an easy way to get bookings...at the end of the week, if they host/hostess accomplishes this; they get that item for a gift. They will be ready to do it again!

Go Diamond
by Using Visuals

Have a clear visual image to look at what you are committed to achieving. Seeing is believing, so draw on the excitement of your goal visually. Share the pictures of what you desire and then visualize yourself in that picture, achieving exactly what you want to achieve. Motivate others to envision their own future successes and watch their businesses grow. Use visual aids that engage the prospects eyes: catalogs, notes, photographs, pictures, presentation manuals, sales kits, recruiting brochures, stories, testimonials, visuals, videos.

- A visual presentation tells your prospect more than you can explain in twice the time by words alone, and much more clearly. Seeing is the most important of the five senses for comprehension.
- If your product presentation or opportunity is lengthy or involved, put it into an outline and put it in a binder.
- Note along with each point the comments or benefit descriptions that will keep the prospects' attention focused on what they get.
- The eyes increase retention possibilities 55%.
- The best presentation is an in-use presentation. Show products as you talk about them.
- When you show a prospect the benefits of using your products, your passions and faith increases their confidence in you.
- When you show a prospect how to use your products or the benefits the prospect will get from using your products, you give the prospect confidence in you; it shows that you have faith in your product.
- While you are outlining your presentation, make sure that you have visuals.
- Visuals stimulate your words. As you train, the prospect sees and understands more.

 Diamond Tip: It's not what you know, it's what you show.

Tips on Showing Videos:
•Act as though you are showing the video for the first time, no matter how often you have seen it.
•Do not show a video that includes outdated information.
•If you show a video or slides, make sure the equipment is working before you start.
•Point out to your prospects beforehand what to look for.
•Summarize at the end and ask for questions.
•Videos are valuable in describing complicated subjects in the shortest time.

Tips for Using Charts and Graphs:
•Charts and graphs can accomplish more in a few seconds than minutes or even hours of recited information.
•Place charts where people can easily see them.
•Rehearse your use of your charts until you can smoothly handle them without awkwardness.
•Take your time showing charts, it will take a person longer to absorb one kind of chart information than another.
•When you present a chart or graph, explain briefly what it shows, or make an explanatory comment.

Tips for Using Photos:
•Pictures are worth 1,000 words.
•A picture of places or people that your prospects or successline knows personally or have heard of, has the greatest power of all.
•Be the one to take pictures and always have film ready.
•Show *"before"* and *"after"* pictures.
•Take lots of photos.

Tips for Using a Presentation Manual:
•At the time you are keeping the prospect's eyes busy, let them see each point as you explain it.
•By going through the manual page by page with the prospect, you can be sure of a thorough, orderly and time-saving coverage of the benefits.
•Make a presentation brief by using a manual.
•Check the prospect's understanding of one point before you proceed to the next.
•Don't let the prospect get ahead of you.
•Don't parrot the prepared manual.
•Don't read the words printed in the manual outloud; say them in your own words.
•Maintain control of the manual and the presentation.

74

•Make every effort to personalize the presentation.
•Practice your presentation using the manual so that you don't stumble
  through the presentation.
•Presentation Manuals are usually intended as a step-by-step guide for the
  presentation.

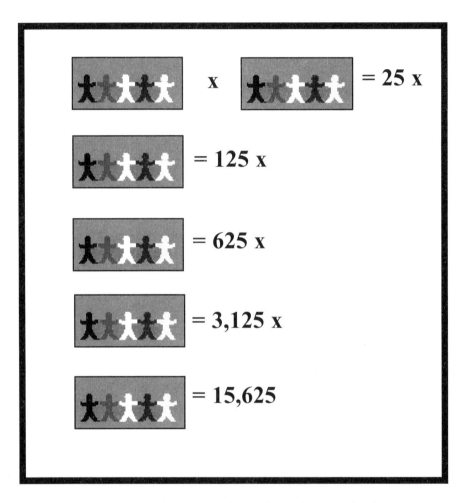

Just start with sponsoring 5 people and get them to do the same.
In the beginning the numbers are small. As your successline grows,
the numbers are huge!

Diamond Tip: Be duplicatable and have people think, *"I can
do this, and I can do it better than you."*

Powerful Sizzle Sessions

A *sizzle session* is getting a group of distributors together to brainstorm ideas and introduce the new members of the team to each other. Distributors catch the energy generated from the other distributors who are already on fire with desire. It's the sizzle, which sells the vision and builds the belief. So how does the sizzle fit into the building of a business? The majority of companies have a training scheduled locally, regionally and nationally. However, there is also **immense** power and synergy in your own group coming together and brainstorming ideas.

Why hold a *sizzle session?*

The *sizzle session* is a very powerful way to help create team identity. The feeling of belonging to a successline and being valued is important. The coming together of a group of like-minded distributors is infectious. Distributors that have the same ideas, goals, visions, wants and needs. They can cheer each other on, share ideas, stories, goals and commitment. The *sizzle session* is a positive, non-threatening environment that allows people to express themselves and to ask questions about details of the compensation plan and get more understanding of what is possible. Distributors become familiar with the details, giving them confidence and allowing them to grow even faster. Instilling this confidence into new distributors will, in turn, help identify new and emerging leaders.

Set up your own recognition and reward program that recognizes distributors in all areas of the business, from selling to sponsoring or reaching a new position on the compensation plan. It's a great way to brainstorm any new ideas or systems that have been put into place, allowing distributors to discuss, feel confident, and then implement them. It gives you, the leader of the session, a chance to inspire your successline, showing them that you believe in them, empowering them with your belief in not only what you are personally achieving but also in what THEY are capable of achieving. *Sizzle sessions* are a very powerful way to propel a business forward. Imagine how your business will grow, when you have the leaders in your successline doing their own *sizzles* each month.

Where should *sizzle sessions* be held?

Start them in the home. This provides a welcoming and relaxing atmosphere to share ideas. There are other alternatives. If you find that your home is not in a convenient location or you cannot accommodate very many people in your home, then use a local hotel reception area, or a room at a local sports center, coffee shop and/or a restaurant; it's really up to you. The *sizzle session* is very effective when people feel relaxed and are more receptive to learning new information. People love the idea of working from home.

How long should the *sizzle session* last?

No longer than an hour and a half.

When to hold a *sizzle session*:

There is no ideal time of the week, day or night, to schedule a *sizzle session*. At least once a month, work it in around your schedule.

There will be all types of people in a successline, with their own time commitments to consider. Have a *sizzle session* in a coffee shop one morning, to take into account distributors who have time during the day but not in the evening? Or have an early evening *sizzle session* to take into account the people who will come for an hour straight after work or then again, an evening *sizzle session*, normally at 8:00 pm. They all work and its great to offer people the choice.

As your successline grows, you may schedule these *sizzle sessions* as regular events and promote them to your successline by group newsletter, voicemail or email loop. It's best to hold them at the same time each month, so people get used to them being held and can schedule themselves to attend.

What to cover at the *sizzle session*?

The basic skills required are all similar, no matter which company. Compensation plans and products will differ but the need to develop skills in talking, recruiting and team building are common to all. The key to building a long-term and residual income is to coach your team to competency in those basics, taking the time to explain and show your new distributors how all the components work and also to coach them to develop a *"have a go"* attitude. The *sizzle session* involves spending no more than an hour-and-a-half together, so it's best to cover a single topic, at most two, at each event.

This will keep the trainer focused and will help the successline get a good understanding on the subject that you have chosen. You can take any subject out of this book and use it in your meetings.

How to start a *sizzle session*?

•Welcome everyone.

•State the purpose of the meeting and how long it will be.

•Encourage everyone to get involved and have some fun.

•Remind everyone that it is a positive meeting and not a place for any negatives. Encourage everyone to take notes and get involved.

•Get each of the team members present to introduce themselves to the group, taking no more than one minute and giving their name, and their reason for having joined your company.

What are some examples of topics to cover at the *sizzle*?

Explain your Compensation Plan at the sizzle: The majority of distributors in any company have never been involved in Network Marketing before and the sight of any plan, with all its numbers, percentages, and peculiar terminologies and jargon, is enough to put them into a mild panic. They may feel *"silly"* for asking questions, or fear being ridiculed. Explaining your Compensation Plan is one of the best topics to speak on, as it's so much fun when you are coaching all the *"ins and outs"* of the plan, taking your time and *"watching the lights go on"* as each person *"gets it"* that they can be very successful. Don't be tempted to rush through this topic, as it's important that distributors believe and can see themselves achieving the positions on the plan. Once distributors grasp the power of what is possible for them to achieve, they will be wanting to race out the door to get on their cell phones and get busy sponsoring, selling and teaching others to do the same.

Always ask for referrals:

Look at your *"chicken list"* in a new way. Learn from distributors who have achieved Diamond in your company. Explain to the prospect that by working smart consistently for a few hours every week, they will be able to replace a six figure income in three to five years; or perhaps generate a larger income than at present. Many prospects will be open minded and receptive to the concepts of time leverage and the possibility of having an unlimited income. Train your distributors to have confidence to share the opportunity and products. Remember, *if you don't ask, you don't get*!

Referrals from your *"Who Do You Know List?"*:

A great *sizzle session* topic is *"How to ask for referrals."* Coach distributors that some people will say, *"No"* to the opportunity. Coach distributors in your successline to learn how to handle rejection. Most prospects are not rejecting the messenger, only the message, so coach people on the ability to to not take rejection personally. They just will not be able to see what you see and that's okay, but please coach your team on how to **ask for the referral**. Why? Almost everyone knows someone, for whom your opportunity would be just great. When making the call to a prospect and they have said that it's *"not for them,"* we don't find out whether that means *"no not ever,"* as against *"no not now,"* or think of asking for referrals.

Use this script, *"Well, I'm really sorry John, that the opportunity isn't for you right now. I actually thought of you as one of the top-10 people I would most like to work with. However, things change so let's keep-in-touch. In the meantime, I am looking for a few key people who are like you with good attitudes and who want to make a 6-figure income. Do you know anyone like that and may I contact them?"*

Almost always, they will tell you they cannot think of anyone, which is a natural reaction to the type of question that has just been asked *"out of the blue,"* so tell them that you would appreciate their help and will give them a call back within 24 hours, to see if they have thought of someone. Then tell them that as a *"thank you"* for their help, you will be sending them a complimentary product.

Powerful Success Tips To
Going Diamond

When you are serious about moving up your Compensation Plan, you will want to repeat what gets results. Make a list of your habits, of your systems, of what works and what doesn't work. Delegate, let others help you; don't try to control everything that goes on, you can't. It's much easier and less stressful to borrow powerful success tips to help you help yourself get up the compensation plan faster. Don't waste precious time on the time wasters or the drain people (those who drain away your lifetime without taking action). Prioritize; don't procrastinate, but allow for distractions. Navigate quickly through the life challenges that will come your way.

Here is what we suggest:
•Attend conferences, meetings, and conventions.
•Be so busy giving recognition that you don't need it yourself.
•Build leaders and make **THEM** successful.
•Conduct regular trainings.
•Create a learning environment.
•Cross off your "to-do" list as you go along.
•Do your calls early in the day.
•Don't play office.
•Duplicate yourself.
•Empower your successline distributors to have a personal growth and development program.
•Encourage distributors to email you regularly with any questions that you can help them ponder and take action upon.
•Encourage teamwork.
•Focus on the positive, be an optimist.
•Get an email loop going with your leaders so you can stay in touch.
•Have a list of phone numbers nearby.
•Have a phone call system (voice mail, weekly or monthly conference call).
•Have paper and pen ready to take notes.
•Have a filing system.
•Have your calendar with you at all times when on the phone.

•Never ask anyone to do something you are not prepared to do yourself.
•Provide information to the team; i.e. Stats, progress, and who is leading the field.
•Recognize team accomplishments.
•Reinforce continuous improvement for the team and yourself.
•Return all phone calls in a timely manner.
•Review your results on a regular basis. *What is working? What is not? What needs to be changed? What needs to be thrown out? What needs to be added or deleted from the way you are building your business?*
•Send welcome letter to each new member of your successline, either via snailmail or email.
•Set goals with new distributors i.e. *"Where do you want to take your business? Do you want to go to the top?"*
•Teach distributors to be trainers and coaches from the beginning.
•Touch a piece of paper only once.
•Touch your business every day.
•Use everyone's creative talents: encourage help with flyers, decorations for meetings.
•Use positive speech.
•Use your incentive trip as a working trip. Meet with your leaders.
•Work from a clean desk.

Delegate:
•Be the upline who gives support and guidance.
•Don't want to and don't need to control all events.
•Get a student to help make up your packages.
•Get leaders involved in planning their own meetings, writing their own newsletters, and making their own decisions.
•Get people to help you do things anyone can do.
•Get your recruits to drive their own businesses, letting them lead.
•Let your children stamp catalogs.
•Let your spouse know how they can help.
•Let up-and-coming stars plan events, meetings and trainings.
•Prepare your leaders to be Diamonds.
•Teach your eagles to fly on their own.
•Your time is better spent moving your business forward.

How to Delegate for Trainings:
Getting others involved in the running of your training will ease your workload and make those you ask to help to feel valued. Everyone has a part to play, and as the saying goes *"TEAM means Together Everyone Achieves More."* Delegation is so important, as it encourages distributors to get

involved, feel valued and be part of the team. All participating distributors should be coached first as to what you want.
•Have someone work the registration table; coach them on how to welcome people.
•Have someone responsible for the music; you may want to discuss your requirements first.
•Have someone setting out the literature and product tables.
•Have someone working the technical equipment.

The Mother Eagle:
•Builds the nest.
•Provides soft cover.
•Lays eggs.
•Nurtures babies.
•Makes them less comfortable.
•Throws the baby out of the nest over and over until the baby can fly.
•Scoops up the baby that isn't ready and tries again, time after time to get the baby to fly.
•Lets the babies fly on their own.

Time Management:
•Manage your 24 hours a day in a smart way.
•You can't stroll to a goal; you must put time into building your successline.
•Divide your successline into the following categories:
    Producers, Average Performers, Low Performers.
•Here is where to spend your time:
    •Producers (top 20-25%) weekly contact.
    •Average Performers (25-75%) bi-monthly contact.
    •Low Performers (bottom 25%) monthly contact.
•Keep a *Daily Inspiration* email going online every day, share great news with your team via email.
•Use your daytimer (filofax, diary).
•Block times when you don't answer the phone.
•Keep each phone call to a maximum of 10 minutes; unless talking with your top producers.

Prioritize your day:
•Call company hotline/voicemail for daily updates.
•Do hostess coaching calls for next week.
•Follow up on recruit leads from last nights (party, demo, show, launch).
•Make 5 new phone calls.
•Make daily lists with realistic goals for the day.
•Send recruit packages to leads.

Don't Procrastinate:
•Wait for the rain, the flowers will die.
•Get busy building your successline; don't wait.
•Two new friends a day brings freedom my way.

Allow for Distractions:
•At any given time, something you least expect may take your focus off your business.
•Allow for challenges with shipments, dates of trainings changing.
•Don't run out or paperwork or catalogs; have plenty on hand.

Eliminate Time Wasters:
•Long drawn out phone calls not going anywhere.
•Forgetting things; use a calendar.
•Shuffling for lost papers; use a spiral notebook.
•Perfectionism.
•Indecision.
•Idle time.
•Self-interruptions.
•Inability to say "*no.*"
•Sleeping longer than necessary.
•Rewriting details.
•No quiet hour without interruptions.
•Filing too much.
•Throwing out too little.
•Too much time on personal and outside activities.
•Day dreaming.
•MBP= Managing by piles.
•Having to run upstairs.
•Looking for glasses or car keys.

87 Ways to Book More Home Parties, Demos, Shows or Launches

There are many ways to book more parties, demos, shows or launches. Get creative. Think of all the ways to promote your business. You are a master promoter and it's up to you to promote your business. You can't just hope that people will line up down your street to knock down your door to get happily involved. It doesn't work that way. Network Marketing is exactly that, Networking. Here are some ideas to start you out on the path to being a master promoter. Take urgent action. Tell everyone what you are doing and ask people for referrals. Have fun in Networkingland! Once you get the hang of it, it's like a train that has left the station. Get serious about taking urgent action to build your business.

1. Advertise in the local printed programs for festivals, school plays, church bazaars, etc.
2. Advertise in your alumni newsletter and/or local newspaper.
3. Advertise in your church bulletin.
4. Ask friends to have a show.
5. Ask friends to help you get started or reach a certain goal.
6. Ask past hostesses at shows to talk about their free products.
7. ASK, ASK, ASK.
8. At the beginning of your show, mention the hostess' goal.
9. Be friendly and enthusiastic.
10. Be prepared to answer questions about what you do.
11. Be willing to share the business opportunity every day.
12. Call anyone who has said *"maybe"* or *"sometime."*
13. Call at least two potential hostesses every day.
14. Call past hostesses.
15. Call potential hostesses who postponed or never booked.
16. Call the most familiar people first.
17. Call your realtor/estate agent with suggestions for *"new home packages."*
18. Carry a notepad to jot down names as you think of them.

19. Contact schools.
20. Do a fundraiser for your favorite charity.
21. Describe and highlight the hostess plan during shows.
22. Do random mailings.
23. Don't be shy talking about your products or your business.
24. Dream big and imagine the possibilities.
25. Encourage frequent customers to regularly plan shows.
26. Encourage hostesses to rebook shows as soon as new brochures or campaigns start.
27. Encourage relatives to book a show.
28. Encourage your hostesses and guests to refer potential hostesses to you.
29. Follow through on every booking lead.
30. Follow up phone calls to particularly interested guests.
31. Get a list of student's parents from private schools.
32. Get more fired up about the possibilities.
33. Give a catalog to the receptionist at your doctor or dentist's office.
34. Give extra service and time to good customers - they will be repeat hostesses and potential distributors.
35. Give products as gifts or donations.
36. Have a booth at a school fair.
37. Have a coffee and ask the parent's of your children's classroom to pop by.
38. Have the hostess tell why she decided to host a show.
39. Have your family members wear a T-shirt or sweatshirt with your logo.
40. Have your husband or significant other promote the products at work.
41. Hold a Christmas Shopping Show for Father's (or for Mother's Day).
42. Hold an opportunity night nearby. Don't wait for someone else to do it.
43. Host your own private showing.
44. Host a show before or during a school meeting.
45. Host an office party or brunch.
46. Include a coupon for a special discount.
47. Include a wrap or flyer with your bill payments.
48. Keep a list of special requests and let those guests know when that product is on sale. Leave your business cards on bulletin boards or in local businesses.
49. Let guests have a catalog or sales brochure to keep on hand or pass it around at work.
50. Mail out samples, catalogs and a wish list.
51. Mention hostess gifts and other benefits at least 3 times per show.

52. Mention how much your *"average"* hostess gets in products.
53. Never promote the least expensive items.
54. New people may be looking for a distributor or a new job in your area.
55. Offer a bonus for hostesses who book on days and/or months when you need an extra show.
56. Offer a holiday wish list to your guests.
57. Offer a Bridal Registry, a Birthday Club, and/or Baby Registry, to let people pick out gifts.
58. Offer to do a class for your local Community College or University.
59. Open a phone book and randomly choose a name.
60. Participate in a school fund-raiser.
61. Post flyers where you can see them.
62. Promote baby showers.
63. Promote Bridal Party shows.
64. Put a catalog in the employee lunchroom.
65. Put a catalog in the teacher's lounge at your child's school.
66. Put an *"ask me about* (name of your company)" button on your handbag or coat.
67. Put current catalog or wrap in your neighbor's door.
68. Read sales, self-improvement, and positive thinking books.
69. Review orders from past shows - guests who have bought frequently, a certain type of item, etc.
70. Send a catalog to a co-worker that has moved.
71. Send a catalog to friends.
72. Set big goals and review them constantly.
73. Set up a display at a craft fair.
74. Set up a display at a mall.
75. Share upcoming specials at shows and during phone calls. Tell prospect that they will be the first to see and try our new products at your next show.
76. Smile when talking on the phone. It'll show through.
77. Spend time every day working on some aspect of your business.
78. Start an e-mail address book of customers who want to know what the monthly specials are, don't forget to mention the Hostess specials. If there isn't one, create one.
79. Suggest hosting a holiday shopping event without having to leave home. Shop from your seat not your feet.
80. Take a catalog to any social meetings you attend.
81. Talk about upcoming specials with everyone.
82. Tell your hostess how much she saved by having her show. She may decide to become a distributor.

83. Treat hostesses to a special *"Hostess Appreciation Tea"* at your home or at a lovely location.
84. Use hostess flyers. Use postcards and/or newsletters to continue to spark interest.
85. Use your products and samples at home, office, camping, parties, etc.
86. Write down names of people who *"owe you a favor,"* then follow up.
87. Write Thank You notes, even if a customer buys nothing or only one item. Sarah White in the U.S.A. booked a web party for over 1,300 people from sending out a thank you note.

> *Stay in opulent accommodations where there is impeccable service. Visit lavish spas, exclusive shops, casinos, cruises and enjoy the very best life the world has to offer. Go Diamond.*

 Diamond Tip: Get your products and opportunity out in front of as many people as possible.

70 Places to Leave Catalogs

Distribute your company catalogs and any recruiting brochures. They are great tools and can make a huge difference in how fast you *Go Diamond*. Invest in a lot of them. Make sure that your name; email address and company distributor number are on every single one of them. If you have a web address where they can order online, make sure you include that as well. Here are some ideas for you to pass out your paperwork and fire up to *Go Diamond*!

1. Accountants/Bookkeppers
2. At ATM machines
3. Airplanes
4. Airports
5. Bagel shops
6. Bakeries
7. Bank tellers
8. Beauty salons
9. Bowling alleys
10. Bus stops
11. Car dealerships
12. College campuses
13. Computer stores
14. Corner stores
15. Counselors
16. Dance studios
17. Day care centers
18. Deli's /Coffee Shops
19. Dental offices
20. Doctor's offices
21. Donut shops
22. Dressings rooms
23. Dry cleaners
24. Fabric stores
25. Flower shops
26. Furniture stores
27. Gas stations
28. Grocery store bulletin boards
29. Grocery store clerks
30. Gyms
31. Hair Salons
32. Health food stores
33. Ice cream shops
34. Insurance offices
35. Investment advisors
36. Laundromats
37. Libraries
38. Magazine holders
39. Mechanic's waiting rooms
40. Medical offices
41. Mortgage offices
42. Movie theater lobbies
43. Nail salons
44. On cars
45. Orthodontist
46. Offices
47. Pet stores
48. Pharmacies
49. Post offices
50. Print shops
51. Public waiting rooms
52. Pubs

53. Real estate offices
54. Restaurants
55. Retirement homes
56. School administration offices
57. Senior citizen activity centers
58. Shoe stores
59. Tanning salons
60. Tax preparation offices
61. Telephone answering services.
62. Temporary staffing offices
63. Tennis clubs
64. Toll booth clerks
65. Travel agency offices
66. Veterinarians offices
67. Video stores
68. Walk-in medical center waiting area
69. With sales personnel at any store
70. With your tip at a restaurant

In the rough, a Diamond barely has a hint of glitter. It is only after the Diamond cutter gets his hands on the unfinished stone, precisely cutting and polishing it, that it dons its shimmer.

Pick Your Paycheck

Decide how much money you want to make. It all depends on your commitment, conviction, determination, and willingness to sell products, recruit others and teach them to do the same.

Here is how:
Help others increase their incomes.
Earn from catalog sales, home parties, demos, shows, or launches.
Bonuses are available; raises come quickly.
Go Diamond!

Get a system that is proven:
•Jan Ruhe and Jayne Leach use *The Go Diamond System*. Both went Diamond using this system.
•Gavin Scott, a top networker in the UK and Ireland, trains distributors to read the following books:

The Basics by Don Failla
The Big Picture by Edward Ludbrook
Fire up! by Jan Ruhe

READERS ARE LEADERS
AND LEADERS ARE READERS

 Diamond Tip: Get a paycheck, not a playcheck.

It's all up to you deciding to decide,
to get the fire of desire.

It starts today!

1. Make a Decision to *Go Diamond*.
2. Feed your mind by getting into a Personal Growth
   and Development Program.
3. Follow those distributors in your company who are
   living the lifestyle you want; who have gone
   Diamond.
4. Use *The Go Diamond System*.
5. Stick with the *Go Diamond* Fundamentals.

Section 2....

Train Yourself

Train Yourself

The gems in this section will help keep the focus on growing the business to get to the top, fast! Go through each of these gems carefully; study them all, apply them and don't miss a single step. This one section will help you *Go Diamond* quicker than you dreamed possible. Here is the information; use it; take urgent action. Your future starts today!

Go to work on yourself.

The faster you follow this advice, the quicker your business will grow. For financial success to occur, personal growth and development must come first.

These gems will be like directed beams of light, to help you reflect upon and consider certain facets of your future success. There are just a few and they brilliantly illuminate the power of inspiring you to help yourself create a business that will pay you residual income for the rest of your life.

Mastering these gems will set you apart from others and will help you to become a Master Trainer. Have an extraordinary ability to get others to become the best they can be. Use your magnetic personality and power to stimulate, reach out and grip others via their senses to becoming professional trainers as well. Be so confident in your training of others, that you radiate confidence and attract people to you. Want distributors to thank you, for giving them the belief and confidence that they too can achieve their dreams.

It all starts with you. If you are getting results, then distributors will want to be coached and trained by you. They will look to you as the guide, the leader and will cherish your training. They will duplicate what works, not what doesn't work. They want you to give them confidence, inspiration and the ability to get results. When you are leading by example, then distributors will want to come and listen intently to what you have to say, because you have something of value that they want to learn.

If you are not leading by example and are not moving towards *Going Diamond*, then it will only be a matter of time before distributors realize that you have little or no useful information to give them. At that time, they will seek information to help them succeed from other sources than you. Keep learning; always be the student.

What makes diamonds so valuable?

Diamonds are the hardest natural substance known to mankind. That, along with the brilliance and fire of diamonds makes them the quintessential symbol of timeless, enduring love. In 1477 AD, Archduke Maximilian of Austria presented a diamond ring to Mary of Burgundy as a sign of their engagement. He put the ring on her third finger of her left hand, the finger believed by ancient Egyptians to have a vein that led directly to the heart. She accepted his proposal and the diamond engagement ring was born. And THAT was duplicatable, wouldn't you agree?

The facts are clear of how to mine diamonds and the system is in place for mining diamonds. More than 250 TONS of ore need to be mined to yield a one-carat rough diamond. There are many steps in getting a diamond ready for marketing. When you decide to *Go Diamond*, there are steps to go through and you are on your way to making a fortune.

There is much to learn on your path to success. Diamonds are self-starters and peak performers. They are massively interested in personal growth and development and go to work on changing themselves. Train yourself as you learn while you earn. Devour this information and revisit it often. Remember, there are *No Limits* to what you can achieve using *The Go Diamond System.* There is a day that you hear about *Going Diamond*, but the day you decide to decide to *Go Diamond* and the decision has been made, you step over the line, you become unstoppable, you set the goal and then …..wild horses can't stop you. *Go Diamond!*

Network Marketing is so exciting and there are so many facets to learn. It all comes together like a sparkling diamond when you put all the gems together. Take urgent action and know that your activity will either expose you or promote you. After becoming a student and taking massive action, you will promote up your compensation plan, fast. You will not be denied, you will be motivated, inspired, focused and you will *Go Diamond*! There will be no choice to look back, turn back or give up or give in…. the day you truly decide to *Go Diamond* will be one of the most important days of your life. All compensation plans are geared to pay those who take the most action and who learn how to get incredible results.

You might have been in Network Marketing for a short time or a very long time. It doesn't matter. Start using this system today so that your success story will be the shining story in your company this year. You deserve to live the lifestyle of a Diamond distributor.

Come to the table of plenty, there is a fortune and an incredible lifestyle waiting for **you** when you *Go Diamond*!

Today is the first day of the rest of your life. Be productive and go for greatness. When you train yourself these key gems and you train others to do the same, and use *The Go Diamond System*, your business should prosper beyond your wildest expectations! Be prepared; prosperity and abundance follow personal growth and development. *Go Diamond!*

This chapter is going to help guide you along your path to *Going Diamond*. It includes all kinds of facets that you will want to make sure you have concentrated on, to help yourself *Go Diamond*. While you are working on mastering them all, be sure and train these ideas over and over and over again.

The drive towards Diamond must be a sustained and continuous effort. Dream of being a Diamond and then be clear that you must do much more than dream it to reach the goal of Diamond. We have really one secret to share. Our sure-fire success formula that we used can be boiled down to six key words:

Hard work makes dreams come true.

> *"That which has carried us through trying periods of our careers, is the psychological factor of always thinking positively and looking forward to the best things happening to us all of the time. It seems to us that if you think negatively, you are conditioning yourself to expect bad things to happen and you usually end up with that. We think back to one saying, which we have both kept in our minds for years: No matter what happens, we cannot expend energy worrying about what people think of us. We have to face challenges head on. To overcome any adversity, all we need is time; we just make sure that all of our steps are forward. Around us, don't ever talk about losing or quitting, have a positive attitude, focus on Going Diamond and believe it will happen."*
> – Jan Ruhe and Jayne Leach

Many people want to *Go Diamond* overnight, but it just doesn't happen that way. Success knows no shortcuts. Masterpieces take time.

There is no promise that if you read this book and follow the System, then you will become a Diamond. By taking action on ideas shared in this book *you will be able to become the best Network Marketer you can be.* You won't have to wonder how good you might have become, because you will know. When you decide to put a high priority on *Going Diamond*, you will be competitive with yourself and others. Too many distributors are afraid of competition. Don't be, not you. Many distributors sneer at success if it requires hard work, training and self-sacrifice.

To succeed, go out and make your own luck. Work harder than others. No matter what stage you are in today in your business, work to improve your skills.

There is no magic formula, just hard work. You must have supreme confidence that you are *Going Diamond*. Get distributors to believe in themselves. The most important priority? Self-confidence. 95% of the people in the world do not believe they have as much talent or ability as other people. It's not talent, looks, intelligence or ability that causes you to believe in yourself. It's asking yourself this very simple question: *"Am I doing the very best I possibly can every day?"*

Get people *to believe in themselves and care about each other.* When you bring a group of people together, it's a start. When you get a group of people to stay together, it's progress. And when you get a group of people to work together, it's success. When you get people to like one another, believe in each other and feel secure within the organization, magic happens.

When you are secure, it's easy to look for the good qualities in building a business. If you don't believe in yourself, if you are constantly looking for the negatives of why you can't *Go Diamond,* there is no chance of you getting there. It all starts with your vision, belief and desire to do what it takes to *Go Diamond.*

Study where this information can fit into your overall goals. All of the messages in this book are pointing you in the same direction:

Go Diamond!

Chapter Four
The 100 + *Go Diamond* Gems

1. *Accept* others
2. Take massive *Action* now
3. Use *Affirmations* daily
4. Be *Accountable*
5. Be careful with whom you *Associate*
6. *Attitude* is everything
7. Have an *Attitude of Gratitude*
8. Be *Available*
9. Strive to have *Balance*
10. Sell the *Benefits*
11. *Bless and Release*
12. *Celebrate* your successes
13. Embrace *Change*
14. Have an unbending *Character*
15. Make *Choices*
16. Be a Master at *Closing Skills*
17. Make a *Commitment*
18. *Communication* is vital
19. Be *Competitive*
20. Have *Confidence* in yourself
21. Reach your goals with *Conviction*
22. *Cooperate*
23. *Concentrate*
24. Be *Consistent*
25. Have *Courage*
26. *Create* the Big-Picture Thinking
27. Be *Creative*
28. Handle *Critics*
29. *Dare* to be Great
30. *Decide* what you wish to achieve
31. *Dedicate* yourself to *Going Diamond*
32. *Define* your Why
33. Have a massive *Desire*
34. It's your fate, your *Destiny*
35. Be *Determined*
36. *Duplicate*
37. Get *Enthralled* in *Going Diamond*
38. Be *Enthusiastic*
39. Be a shining *Example*
40. *Expect* Miracles
41. Explain your *Expectations*
42. Learn from *Failure*
43. Be *Fair*
44. Have *Faith*
45. Have an unshakeable *Faith*
46. Overcome *Fear*
47. Use *Feel, Felt, Found*
48. Be *Flexible*
49. *Forgive* those who hurt you
50. Make this your decade of *Fun*
51. Focus on the *Fundamentals*
52. Set massive *Goals*
53. Go for *Greatness*
54. Be a *Hope Coach*
55. Be *Honest*
56. *How* to do the Business
57. Be an *Inspiration*

58. *Invest* in yourself
59. Gather *Knowledge*
60. Take the *Leap*
61. Do not be afraid of *Leading*
62. *Leave* Something Behind
63. Prepare for *Loneliness*
64. Be *Loyal*
65. The *Magic Lamp*
66. *Motivation* comes from within
67. Handle the Word *"No"*
68. *Nuture Others*
69. Handle *Objections*
70. Lead with the *Opportunity*
71. *Opportunity* is knocking
72. Stay *Optimistic*
73. Get *Organized*
74. Be in *Partnership*
75. Live with *Passion*
76. Have *Patience* and *Stick-to-it-tiveness*
77. *Persistency*
78. Have a *Personal Growth* and Development Program
79. Make a *Plan*
80. *Practice*
81. Take *Personal Responsibility*
82. Work on your *Presentation*
83. Thrive on *Pressure*
84. Take *Pride* in what you are accomplishing
85. Master *Prospecting*
86. Master *Recruiting*
87. Never, ever, *Quit*
88. Be busy giving *Recognition*
89. Handle *Rejection*
90. Take *Risks*
91. *Sacrifices*
92. Be *Self-Motivated*
93. *Simplify* your business
94. Improve your *Skills*
95. Study *Successful* People
96. Handle *Success*
97. The major key to *Success*
98. *Survival*
99. Use the *SWSWSW... NEXT... SW* formula
100. The *Time* Has Come
101. Be *Trainable*
102. *Teamwork* Gems
103. Be *Unselfish*
104. Have a clear *Vision*
105. Have pure *Zeal*

It takes but one positive thought,

when given a chance to surive and thrive,

to overpower an entire army of

negative thoughts.

Go *Diamond Gems*

1. *Accept* others:

Accept distributors who have different cultures, political beliefs or religious beliefs. Accept people as they are and do not try to change them to believe like you do. You can't change anyone; you can only change how you react to them. Welcome people unlike you into your successline; learn from them.

2. Take massive *Action* now:

Take massive urgent action. Make a plan, plan to work and then work your plan. Don't just dream about what you will plan to do, don't just talk about what you plan to do; don't just write down what you plan to do, **take action.** No one jumps on your bandwagon until you get it going.

3. Use *Affirmations* daily:

Listen to what you are saying in your head to yourself. Replace all negative thoughts with positive ones all day long.

4. Be *Accountable*:

Be accountable. If you say you are going to achieve a certain level, work to get it. Show up for the meetings; let people know that you are doing what you say you are going to do. Be a part of the successline growth.

5. Be careful with whom you *Associate*:

Never seek advice or guidance from anyone who doesn't already have what you want, since they are unqualified to help or advise you. Associate with leaders and *become known by the people you avoid.*

6. *Attitude* is everything:

Expect the best and you'll get it. Expect the worst; you'll get it. Your mental attitude determines your outcome.

7. Have an *Attitude of Gratitude:*

Every morning, when you wake up, say a few words of appreciation for freedom in your life, for choices you get to make during the day, for your loved ones, for the opportunity to *Go Diamond*, for the involvement you have, the contribution you get to make, for your family and for the chance to make a difference.

8. Be *Available*:

Be available to sell, recruit/sponsor, and teach others to do the same. Be available for meetings, conference calls, rallies, luncheons, trainings, planning sessions, celebrations and conventions. Be available and willing to invest the time needed to make Network Marketing work.

9. Strive to have *Balance* in your life:

Have a life. Don't let your business consume you to the point that you neglect yourself or your family. Work for balance in all areas of your life. Take time for yourself and those you love while at the same time building a business.

10. Sell the *Benefits*:

People want to own, not buy. They like to earn big money, free time potential, extra income and a new and better lifestyle. That's what people buy first. Then they will be interested in joining your company as a vehicle to get them what they really want. Once you have many people believing in your opportunity and products and that they can achieve THEIR goals in your company, you will have a thriving business. Just sell the benefits of how they can achieve greatness in your company. The average distributor spends only a few hours a day working face-to-face selling. Each presentation must waste no time nor include any wasted words. Sell the benefits and then sell them some more!

11. Learn to *Bless and Release* with ease:

When you first sponsor someone, they are dependent on you for information, direction and support. They will often become independent; coaching and teaching others on the information you share with them. Some of these people want to be the only upline that people look to for guidance so they make you feel, and they act as if, you are no longer important to them or to the growth of their businesses. You might encounter some people who are jealous, critical, condemning and disloyal, which can be very destructive and upsetting. Bless and release them. Shine your light on those who do want your leadership.

12. *Celebrate* your successes:

Along the way, celebrate your achievements. Celebrate small achievements of people in your successline. Everyone loves to celebrate, have picnics, potluck dinners, and call emergency meetings to celebrate. Think about others' achievements and be the one who helps plan the celebration. Never hesitate to celebrate. There are a lot of achievements on the path to Diamond. Celebrate them all!

13. Embrace *Change*:

Count on one thing *Going Diamond*. Change. You will change, others around you will change, your surroundings will change, and your opinions will change. Embrace change; don't fear it.

14. Have an unbending *Character:*

Character shines with honesty, respect, true humility and an inner faith.

15. Make *Choices:*

Make the choice that you will choose not to be distracted, that you will not let others choose for you. Success is simply a matter of choice.

16. Be a Master at *Closing* Skills:

It doesn't matter how much you know, how polished your presentation is, how enthusiastic you are, how much you love your product, *if you can't ask for the order, or for someone to join your business, it will not grow.* Spend a lot of time in training your distributors on closing skills. Distributors are all fired up after meetings and trainings and conventions and seminars and go out into the world and share their excitement and belief. But what if no one joins them? They get discouraged. Teach them to say:

"Are you ready to get started right now?"

"What information do you need to make a final decision to join today?"

"My company has given me the responsibility to find 5 key people in this area this week; would you be interested in being one of those 5?"

"If you are not interested, please level with me and at least give me some names of people in your life."

Teach these scripts, drill them into the heads of your distributors, make them learn them. Watch their confidence increase. Practice, drill, and rehearse these words.

17. Make a *Commitment* to *Go Diamond* and don't give up:

Once you make the decision and truly commit to *Going Diamond*, wild horses can't stop you!

18. *Communication* is vital:

Connect with people in your successline by email, voicemail, newsletters, videos, postcards, and phone. **Here are 3 ways to increase your recruiting by using your communication skills:** Tell the story, tell the story, tell the story of your opportunity over and over.

19. Be *Competitive*:

Network Marketing thrives on healthy competition between distributors, as they have fun, striving for career progression and to perform at their best. In the majority of companies, there will be top distributor and incentive awards. Leaders should always strive to compete and achieve, leading their successline by the example of their personal results.

20. Have *Confidence* in yourself:

Leaders have the confidence to inspire followers to become leaders. Have the confidence that you will *Go Diamond,* no matter what.

21. Reach your goals with *Conviction*:

When you truly believe in something, when you have conviction, stand firm. Stand up for what you believe even if it's uncomfortable because your successline will see you as a strong leader *Going Diamond*. Most people don't want to cause any commotion, so they just let things go. It's empowering to stand firm for what you believe in and the communication to others is that you won't be taken advantage of. Think great thoughts, plan big goals, and work on projecting your voice with confidence and self worth. Smile and act as if you have reached your goal.

22. *Cooperate*:

Cooperation and teamwork are an infinite power source. When you are involved in a successline you will celebrate achievements together, your successes will be more fun, and your joys bigger and better. When you face tough times, tough decisions, or come to a discouraging time in your business, others will uplift you and care about you and will encourage you to not give up, give in, or be defeated. You can only accomplish Diamond when you work together with your successline. It takes all the instruments to make an orchestra. It takes the orchestra to make a symphony.

23. *Concentrate*:

It's easy to concentrate when everything is going great. Diamonds are the ones who concentrate when they are staring defeat in the face. Concentrate hard on your goals. All your worrying and complaining is not going to change what happened five minutes ago. You can only change what will happen next. Focus on that. Don't look back. Don't brood. Don't complain. Don't worry or wonder if you are ever going to get there. Focus your concentration on what you can do now and forget the past, it simply does not exist any more. Don't stew; do!

24. Be *Consistent*:

No matter how few hours you have each day for your business, follow your plan and use those hours wisely. Believe in what you are doing. You will reap what you sow. If you are consistent, you will work on your business every day, rain or shine. You will study and learn what it takes to build a large organization month after month, year after year.

25. Have *Courage:*

Desire is your wishbone. Courage is your backbone. Your backbone gives you the courage, the get-up-and-go, the guts to achieve, the incentive to make any dream you dare to dream come true. Courage precedes great activity. Courage precedes decision-making. The greatest risk in life is not having the courage to go for our dreams.

26. *Create* the Big-Picture Thinking:

Would you rather make 25% + on your own efforts or 3%+ on the efforts of thousands? Do the math.

27. Be *Creative:*

Use your talents and your creativity. Let your creativity flow. Be open to your creative side. Don't be afraid to try something new, something fresh, and exciting. You are safe to be creative in Network Marketing.

28. Handle *Critics:*

If you are successful, people will be jealous of and criticize you. Don't let them distract you from reaching your goal. It's easy to criticize other people, but it's hard to duplicate their efforts. Critics aren't the leaders or doers in life. The leaders and the doers are too busy with their own accomplishments to criticize.

29. Dare to be *Great*:

Begin today to blaze a path and leave a trail for others to follow. Make a gigantic contribution to building a huge successline.

30. *Decide* what you wish to achieve:

Really ponder and think about what you are willing to work for and get to work achieving it.

31. *Dedicate* yourself to *Going Diamond*:

Being dedicated is being devoted. Dedication is consistent concentration and focus on *Going Diamond.* There are unseen situations that come up to distract you from your focus, but stay dedicated to *Going Diamond* and you will get there. Dedicate yourself to be the student of people living the lifestyle you want to have. Dedicate yourself to being the student of the people getting the results you want. Surround yourself with people who are going to the top, at the top and living the lifestyle you want. Be dedicated to your goal. Dedicate yourself to *Going Diamond* in a reasonable time. It starts today!

32. Define your *Why*:

The *"Why"* is a goal and the journey must be planned very carefully. Think about your goals most of your day and continue to move toward that which is your clear goal. Decide exactly what you want to achieve, write those goals down in a specific way, and set a deadline for the attainment of each goal. What will get you out of bed in the morning to get to work? That is your *"why."*

33. Have a massive *Desire* to *Go Diamond:*

It's amazing what happens when you get a burning desire. Only the truly dedicated distributors ever come close to attaining their goals. They won't let anything interfere with their goals. That's why there are so few Diamonds.

34. It's your fate, your *Destiny*:
Going Diamond is a choice. An amazing future awaits you. When you choose to *Go Diamond,* know that this could certainly be when fate takes a turn for you to have a fabulous future.

35. Be the most *Determined* distributor you know:
Be the most determined person you know to *Go Diamond*. Determination, persistence, consistency and dedication are all part of being mentally prepared to *Go Diamond*. Not many people get to the top *of anything*. There are only so many people at the top. They made the choice to get determined to propel themselves up the compensation plan and would not stop until they got there. When you are determined, you will take risks, you will be relentless and ethical, you will stay fired up, you will do till you drop, you will let others see your determination by your actions and activity. You will do extraordinary things because you are determined. Have the *determination to succeed, the persistence to keep at it and the "never ever give up" attitude.*

36. *Duplication*:
Learning how to teach and train others to sponsor and sell products is essential. That begins the process of the multi-levels you get paid on. Train distributors how to sponsor and train those distributors; who in turn coach their new distributors how to do the same. For example, if you sponsor Bill and coach him how to sponsor Alice, to sponsor Mike, the duplication process has begun. Use *The Go Diamond System* to get massive results.

NDAOPCC: This stands for *Never Do Anything Other People Can't Copy*. Make sure that what you do, others can copy, can duplicate and be successful too.

37. Get *Enthralled* in *Going Diamond*:
Get absolutely enthralled. Throw yourself totally into it with all you have. Your attitude and decision makes the difference.

38. Be *Enthusiastic:*
Radiate enthusiasm, excitement, a fired up attitude, and be the bright shining star that you are.

39. Be a shining *Example* of what is possible:
Model the Diamonds who have gotten results. They have great credibility

and influence with distributors in their successline. You can give all the inspirational speeches you want, but if the rest of the distributors in your organization don't see you putting forth your best effort every single day, they won't either.

40. *Expect* Miracles:

Don't be surprised by miracles, expect them. Nothing happens by chance. When you make a decision to *Go Diamond*, the universe will rearrange itself to accommodate that goal. People will come into your life, not by accident, but on purpose to help you along your path. Books, CD's, audiotapes and seminars that are full of ideas will help you to the top. Use your mentors' wisdom and prepare for prosperity and abundance. Miracles happen every moment on earth. Be ready and be open to them, for they are headed your way.

41. Explain your *Expectations* up front:

When people first get involved, it is important to them to find out what is expected of them and what kind of training they can expect to get, beginning and ongoing. Here are the ***basic expectations*** to train in every training:
   •sell product weekly.
   •sponsor at least one person a month.
   •train those you sponsor to sell, sponsor and train their recruits.

42. Learn from *Failure*:

Yesterday is over, five minutes ago is over. Learn from your past mistakes. Everyone makes mistakes. No one is perfect. If you have failed, let that failure be your teacher. Never see failure as true failure but only as a learning experience. Let failure motivate you, not paralyze you. If you have failed before in another company or business, start anew, find a company you can believe in and try again. If at first you don't succeed, try, try and try again.

43. Be *Fair*:

Do unto others…Treat everyone as you want to be treated. Be fair in how you treat your leaders. Care, share, and be fair.

44. Have *Faith*:

Be faithful to your goals and dreams. Do not be denied. When you have big faith; big things happen to you. No matter how slow your business is going, have faith. All you have to do is believe, work like you have never worked before and *never, never, never quit.*

45. Have an unshakable *Faith* in yourself:

Believe in yourself, the Network Marketing Industry, your products and opportunity.

46. Overcome *Fear:*

Attach more fear to not *Going Diamond* than to *Going Diamond*. Fear is not a limitation; it is only the edge of your comfort zone. There are *No Limits!* Concentrate on *helping other people be successful.*

47. Use the *Feel, Felt, Found* formula:

In conversations, learn to listen carefully to what people say. Then you can say with a great deal of confidence and in an encouraging way, *"I know how you feel, I felt that way too, but NOW I have found..."*

48. Be *Flexible*:

Be prepared to take a fresh approach. Don't hold on to old, outdated ideas that don't get results. If what you are doing is not advancing you toward *Going Diamond*, stop and look at your options for getting there another way. The definition of insanity is doing the same thing over and over again, expecting different results. Check out all the options that you have. Be adaptable. So many distributors have trouble with this because they hate change. They want to debate everything and have trouble moving into uncharted waters. Be the leader who is flexible.

49. *Forgive* those who hurt you:

Forget and forge ahead.

50. Make this your decade of *Fun:*

We are just big children playing a game. Love playing and love the thrill of going to the top. When people go to a baseball game, they don't hear *"work-ball,"* they shout *"play ball!"*

51. Focus on the *Fundamentals:*

• Use the products and love them.
• Share them with other people.
• Sponsor others into the business.
• Coach them how to do the same.

52. Set massive *Goals*:

A goal is just a dream with a deadline. When you set a goal, put it in writing and have a date that it will be achieved, **no matter what**. Set goals and be prepared. It wasn't raining when Noah built the ark. Set massive goals and expect massive results.

53. Go for *Greatness:*

Move beyond being average. Being average is the best of the worst and the worst of the best. Choose to not be average. Being average puts you as close to the bottom as it does to the top. Ordinary people who take extraordinary actions go to the top. Go for greatness and accept nothing less.

54. Be a *Hope Coach:*

One of the greatest gifts you can give others is hope. When giving others hope that their desires are attainable, they will have faith and belief in you to lead them. The great news is that they will be coachable and will follow you.

55. Be *Honest*:

It's just as easy to be honest as it is to be dishonest. Honesty is a quality you must acquire to *Go Diamond,* and for the rest of your life, if you are going to succeed.

56. *How to* do the Business:

People don't want to just believe they can *Go Diamond*, they want to learn how, they want to listen to people who can guide them, coach them and help them *Go Diamond.* They are hungry for information. They want the skills and want to learn them fast. They don't want to mess around at the bottom of the compensation plan. They want to increase their business, their checks and their lifestyle. They search for experts, they listen in to conference calls, and they go to the seminars to pick up just one new idea to try. They are ready to learn and excited to learn how to do the business. It's important to seek out people who have actually succeeded in the business. Read their books and attend their seminars. Stick to the fundamentals.

57. Be an *Inspiration*:

Inspiration is everywhere. Get inspired. It's never too late to get inspired. You can get inspiration from a book, a tape, a video, a seminar, a meeting, around a dinner table, in a church, in a movie, listening to a song or just taking a walk. Light the way for others; be a candle in the darkness, show the way, go the way and be the inspiration for others to follow. Keep your spirit strong; be the sparkling Diamond that others want to follow. We all have someone who has inspired us in our lives. Many teachers will come into your life to make a difference. Be the guide who inspires others.

58. *Invest* in yourself:

Most people do not take the time or trouble to invest in themselves. It's vital to do so; in fact it's essential. Invest in self-improvement, for an investment in your mind is the best investment in the world. Once knowledge is gained, no one can steal it from you. Personal growth and self-knowledge promote self-confidence and belief and once you have confidence and belief, you will be unstoppable.

59. Gather *Knowledge*:

Build your own personal library. Read books, listen to tapes, and go to seminars led by people who are living the lifestyle you want to have. Build your vocabulary.

60. Take the *Leap:*

Leap into the future with the goal to get to *Go Diamond*. Push yourself to the limit. Stretch the envelope. Don't ask for permission to *Go Diamond*. Do what needs to be done to get there. Do *something*, take the leap.

61. Do not be afraid of *Leading*:

Be excited about having a huge organization. It is fun to be the leader. Step out and begin leading today by prospecting, selling, recruiting, training and teach your distributors to do the same. Give people direction on how to get to their destination. Bring out the best in others and help others become leaders. It's a *must to* **use a simple system that others can duplicate.**

62. *Leave* Something Behind:

Leave your company and distributors with memories of a true champion who cared enough for this industry to give something back. Take your knowledge, experience and enthusiasm, and share it with new distributors just getting started. Teach them everything you were taught about *Going Diamond*. Teach them how to lead, teach them about how to overcome adversity and how to ignore the critics.

63. Prepare for *Loneliness* at the Top:

Diamonds are rarely alone. But many leaders at the top are lonely. It's important to take care of your relationships when you are on the journey to Diamond.

64. Be *Loyal*:

If you are not loyal, your organization will not be loyal to you. Always lift up people, don't knock them down. Never say anything unkind about your upline or distributors in your successline.

65. The *Magic Lamp:*

Ask for what you want. Ask people to join you. Ask people who they know who might want to join you. Ask, ask, ask. Ask and you shall receive, seek and you shall find, knock and the door will be opened. It's the philosophy that if you ask enough people to join you, some will, some won't, so what, next, someone is waiting. (SWSWSW…next..SW). This formula works! Share your goal with others that you are *Going Diamond*. Follow your heart and live your dream as a Diamond. Success does not come from a magic lantern, a fairy godmother, fairies, leprechauns, angels or genies. *Going Diamond* comes from asking enough people to join you, then training them on the product and opportunity and how to bring others into the business and to teach them to do the same.

66. *Motivation* comes from within:

Motivation keeps you going. No one can motivate you. Most people can't stay motivated to get to the top. The fastest way to get motivated is to dream, get a goal and make a decision to achieve that dream. Develop the habit of getting up each morning motivated to *Go Diamond*. Instead of saying *"I can't,"* say *"I must."* Turn your *shoulds* into *musts*. Pretend you have the most important person in the world greeting you every day to say, *"I am here watching you and I am so proud of what you are becoming and what you are achieving."*

67. Handle the Word *"No"*:

There will be people who say *"No"* to either or both your opportunity and/or products. Most people hate the rejection because they believe passionately in their opportunity and/or products. *"No"* is just a part of the process of finding people who see the benefits for them. Imagine you had ten guests in your home and offered everyone a glass of water and three said *"No."* Could you handle that? Network Marketing works in exactly the same way. Don't take *"No"* personally. Take the view that you are only the messenger delivering the message and they are rejecting the message, not you. Sometimes when you maintain effective communication, a *"No"* can turn into a *"Yes,"* because the prospect's circumstances have changed.

68. *Nurturing* Others:

Many leaders think they have to nurture new distributors by being on the phone with them constantly, becoming their best friend, letting them confide, sharing their past mistakes and hurts and generally spending a lot of time with them. Here is what is important: teaching people how to recruit, sell, train, prospect, work on their leadership skills and presentation skills, teach and coach how to get to the top, organizational skills, how to be a good listener, drawing the best out of people, showing people how to do the business, the opportunity, sharing the benefits of the products, personal growth, time freedom, not having to conform, being creative, bonding, friendshipping and team building. There is no other business in the world where your success is generated by the more you help others succeed. It's about having integrity of being fair to everyone, equal opportunity for all, helping others succeed beyond their wildest expectations. It's about everyone winning and succeeding. It's about giving back to our communities and giving back to those who helped us get where we are today.

69. Handle *Objections*:

When people give you an objection, know that it is just a stall. They are thinking about what you are saying. Train distributors *how to* answer all of the objections so that they can recruit/sponsor more people or sell more products. Make a list of all the objections that people hear and go over and over and over how to handle them at your meetings and trainings.

Invest in books with scripts on how to handle objections. Suggestion: (MLM Nuts $ Bolts by Jan Ruhe available at www.janruhe.com)

70. Lead with the *Opportunity*:

Sponsor people by sharing what the opportunity can bring them. Have a strong belief in your opportunity and sell the dream. If you are not making exceptional money yet, just tell the story of the people in your company who **are** making the money, living the lifestyle and teaching others how they can achieve the same.

71. *Opportunity* is Knocking:

When opportunity knocks, pay attention. Take a risk to find out if you are on the right path. Sometimes you will succeed, sometimes you won't, but if you don't take action on the opportunity, for sure you will not succeed. There are opportunities everywhere. You alone are responsible for creating your own future. Luck is spelled WORK. When an opportunity presents itself, go for it, don't wait, take urgent action! Every single event in life, however troubling or difficult, conceals opportunity.

72. Stay *Optimistic*:

Optimists see the glass half full, not half empty. Optimists know that tough times never last but tough people do. Optimists know that they are going to have to handle fascinating people, difficult people, people who reject them, people who want to be their best friend, people who are not easy to get along with, and so much more. When things go wrong, as they sometimes will, when you want to give up and quit, get optimistic about the future and stay focused, *Go Diamond*. Keep your focus; do not be distracted by the naysayers. Most critical people stay away from optimistic people. Want to hang out with champions? Be optimistic! Optimism doesn't mean that your climb to Diamond will be easy or perfect. It does mean that you can imagine getting there and can visualize yourself already there. It is in the most dire tragedies and difficulties that our optimism must shine through. Optimists live longer. Optimism gives the hope of a fabulous future in the face of uncertainty. After all, you get to write a happy ending when you *Go Diamond.* Shrug off, and shake off the conventional wisdom about what's possible and what's impossible and turn a deaf ear to the critics. Go ahead and attempt the impossible and succeed far more often than you would think.

73. Get *Organized:*

Throw out clutter. Use your computer, palm computer, manila folders, baskets, filing cabinets, calendars, spiral notebooks or any system that works for you, so that you are not always looking for something that you have misplaced.

74. Be in *Partnership* with your leaders*:*

The distributor who sponsors someone into the business is very very important. Be a partner with people you sponsor; make them feel you are doing the business together.

75. Live with *Passion*:

Passion in this business is incredible. Leading, making a difference, watching others succeed, earning rewards, traveling the world on incentive trips, meeting new people, celebrating achievements and exciting times as a member of a great successline brings out total passion in many distributors. It's fun and passionate people are attracted to Network Marketing every moment of the day. Dreamers come by the thousands with hope of a better future. Talented, successful people who want to get passionate about a hope for a better tomorrow, flock to Network Marketing. Energetic, passionate people want to have a chance at *Going Diamond*. Distributors are attending seminars, reading books and studying so that they can ignite their passion into a roaring bonfire of success to *Go Diamond*. Live with passion the rest of your life.

76. Have *Patience* and *Stick-to-it-iveness*:

Going Diamond takes time. Have patience and don't quit before the payday. Get a paycheck, not a play check. It requires self-discipline, self-control and self-motivation to *Go Diamond*. Treat your business like a business and it will reward you like a business should. If you treat it like a hobby, it will cost you money like most hobbies do. Most distributors are not patient. They want their initial activity to pay off fast. Normally this does not happen. *In the early years, you get paid very little for doing a lot, and in the later years,* **you get paid a lot for doing very little.**

77. *Persistence*:

Keep getting up after being knocked down. Just because a person has failed once or twice or many times, please don't label that person as a failure. Sometimes immediate dreams are temporarily shattered. Champions possess dreams that live. Champions outlive circumstances, challenges and setbacks. Setbacks just make room for comebacks. Success does not come overnight. Success takes being persistent day after day, month after month, and year after year.

78. Have a *Personal Growth* and *Development* Program:

Feed your mind. Readers are leaders and leaders are readers. Get to seminars, become a student, turn your car into a classroom, listen to CD's and audiotapes. Build your own library, **never loan out books and tapes.**

79. Make a *Plan*:

Make a plan of how you intend to *Go Diamond*. How many people do you need to recruit? How many people do they need to recruit? How much in sales must you have? What is the structure that you need to get to the Diamond level? Who can help you learn the skills to get there faster? Then, get the skills you need. Earn while you learn. Learn from distributors who have been trained by a Diamond.

80. *Practice*:

Practice never makes perfect. Practice makes permanent. Practicing prospecting, recruiting, selling, leading, presentation skills, training and going for greatness, become a part of your life and it becomes easy for you to demonstrate to others how to do the same.

81. Take *Personal Responsibility*:

Be responsible to follow up, to be coachable, to coach others. Success or failure in life is up to you. Don't blame others for your situation. You are responsible for what happens in your life. It's the set of the sails, not the wind, that blows people off course.

82. Work on your *Presentation*:

Practice, drill and rehearse your presentation. Learn some key words to use during your presentation of how the products and opportunity will benefit the listener. Sell the benefits of working with you, your company, your products and your opportunity. Polish your presentation skills. Learn how to answer objections. Keep your presentations to 20-30 minutes maximum. Ask questions every five sentences. Example:

"How does this sound so far?" and
"Would you like to join today?" ask,
"Who is responsible for making the final decision?"

Invest in books with scripts on how to improve your presentation skills. Suggestion:
(The Master Presentation Guide by Jan Ruhe available at www.janruhe.com)

83. Thrive on *Pressure*:

Pressure separates the average distributor from the Diamond. Diamonds learn how to handle pressure. When pressure mounts, Diamonds love it, because they are being tested. They thrive on pressure; average distributors fear it.

Diamonds thrive on chaos. If you bring chaos into a Diamonds life, they can handle it and will handle it and come through it just fine. They know that it's just a temporary situation and that there is always opportunity in chaos. When you learn the skills to *Go Diamond*, you won't worry about pressure. Go out of your way to put yourself into pressure situations. You'll thrive on competing with others in your company to be number one. If you don't have faith in what you are doing and you fear the unexpected, you are not prepared. All pressure is self-inflicted; it comes from within. You are in control of how you handle pressure. Average distributors cringe under pressure, for they are not prepared to do their best ever, even when the Upline counts on them. **Welcome pressure**. Look at pressure as an opportunity to show what you can accomplish. If you welcome pressure, you will be amazed at how successful you will be. When under pressure, just slow down your pace, go back to the fundamentals and concentrate. Block everything else out of your mind. Stay cool. Slow down. Get your confidence back. Then face the pressure head on. Don't hide from pressure situations; **look for them.** All of us get knocked down occasionally, but it's the resiliency of getting back up that matters. All of us do well when things are going well, but the thing that distinguishes Diamonds is their ability to do well in times of great stress, urgency and pressure.

84. Take *Pride* in what you are accomplishing:

Take pride in being the best you can be. Pride builds a foundation of courage that allows you to take risks to be better than the rest. The road to *Go Diamond* is not easy, but if you have pride in yourself, you will get there. When you reach your goal, be proud. You paid the price to get there. You deserve to be excited, happy and to celebrate.

85. Master *Prospecting*:

Be a master at prospecting and follow up, follow up, follow up. Sometimes when you are recruiting and you get rejected, you must not get discouraged. People will not join you for thousands of reasons. It only takes a few to get involved to have explosive growth. Master recruiting. Teach others how to recruit from the day they join. Sort through the public; new people are waiting to be recruited by you. Just like a person looking for diamonds in a riverbed, search through the public for people who want to join the business and teach others to do the same. We don't want to beg people to join, we want to offer an opportunity in such a way that people can see the immediate value to their lives. Exit your home and talk to everyone. Ask everyone if they know people who would be interested in making some extra money working part time out of their home. Be prepared for thousands of *"no's,"* it only takes a few people to start an incredible successline.

86. Master *Recruiting*:

You want thousands of distributors each doing a little bit. Thousands. It all starts with duplicating yourself several times. The lifeblood of the business is recruiting. Sponsor/recruit enough people to help the networking process begin to grow. It can only be a few or it might take you several or even many. The numbers are small in the beginning, you reach two, they reach two and now you have four. Train distributors to prospect by asking everyone:

> ### *"Who do they know?*
> ### *Where do they live?*
> ### *How can I reach them?"*

Sponsoring is the driving force to build a large successline. It's essential to sponsor on a consistent basis. With it you will get a *"seed bed"* from which to develop the *"mighty oaks,"* the future leaders in your successline. Never quit sponsoring. Just recruiting someone is not enough; you must help those recruits to be the best they can be. Be a great sponsor of future giants in your company.

87. Never, ever, *Quit*:

When you want to quit, that's the time to start all over again. Stick around for the payday.

88. Be busy giving *Recognition*:

Be so busy giving recognition that you don't need it.

89. Handle *Rejection*:

Going Diamond is not easy. It is a decision. There is rejection along the way. Rejection of your dreams, your products or opportunity, and rejection of your leadership from time to time. Some rejections are hard to shake off. Most are blessings in disguise. Despite the heartbreak of some rejections, press on. Expect people to say *"yes"* to your opportunity, and don't let them discourage you or distract you. No matter what rejections you face while *Going Diamond*, you can overcome them if you ask enough people to help you and give them a good reason for doing so.

90. Take *Risks*:

Ask for what you want in life. Don't be afraid to fail. Your biggest failure may lead to your greatest success. Stop playing it safe and go for greatness. Learn to laugh at yourself and push yourself to go further than you think you can go. Dare to accept that you can be great, that you can *Go Diamond*. Do the unexpected. Set the goal to be the top recruiter in your area or in your country. Step up to the plate, take your foot off the brakes, and get into high gear. Don't let anyone kill your dream. Go against the flow, live in the moment more frequently and don't let small hurts or the critics slow you down. Let criticism motivate you to take more risks. Navigate through tough times. Exude confidence and have an inner glow. Practice introducing yourself with this sentence:

"I am a Diamond!"

91. You might have to make *Sacrifices*:

There are no easy ways to *Go Diamond*. If it was easy, everyone would *Go Diamond*. Hard work's constant companion is sacrifice.

> *"We have wondered what would have happened to us if we had been convinced by the theory of working an eight hour day, leaving our children in daycare, or letting a man solely provide for us would have been a better choice of a life path to take? What if someone had convinced us that it was not fair to our fellow women to put forth our best efforts in our work in Network Marketing and to stay average? We are so thankful that we did not choose a path of mediocrity. We were both single mothers and did not want to leave our children for someone else to raise. That was not an option. If we had opted to go to work and leave our children, if we had stayed average and had not made the effort and not made the sacrifices, we would never have been able to provide the lifestyle that our families are enjoying today."*
>
> – Jan Ruhe and Jayne Leach

92. Be *Self-Motivated*:

Personal success goes beyond self-motivation. Self-motivation is essential to begin the path to the top. Enthusiasm and motivation gets you to the starting line and it is self-motivation that gets you beyond the finish line, and to the top. To stay self-motivated, keep a clear vision of your destiny and be inspired by the prospect of the end result, your outcome.

93. *Simplify* your business:

Get focused only on *Going Diamond* and on your family. Don't take on charity or church responsibilities while *Going Diamond*. There will be lots of time later in your life to be the room mother, the Sunday school teacher, and the Scout leader. Say *"No"* to everything that does not guide you to *Go Diamond*. Clear clutter out of your desk, your handbag, and your car.

94. Improve your *Skills and Techniques*:

For things in your life to change for the better, you must change. Apply new ideas and techniques and be willing to open your mind and learn them. When we communicate effectively, we can make a fortune. People who follow *The Go Diamond System* can expect excellent rewards. Average presentations pay average rewards and poor presentations pay nothing. Develop your skills and techniques to get top rewards. Develop the best techniques you can, then pass them on to your leaders and success is inevitable.

95. Study *Successful* People:

Success breeds success. Walk in the footsteps of someone who has gone before and achieved what you want. There are highly successful distributors who have reached the top by studying the business from the masters that walked before them. Watch them work, observe the way they communicate and work with their successlines. Look at the way they have developed their attitude, focus, vision and passion. Study them and emulate them. Associating with successful distributors will empower you; you will begin to believe in yourself and in the possibilities of achieving your dreams and goals. You will have more confidence and will be clearer on how you are going to achieve your goals. Become a more focused distributor, the kind that others will want to be around. Consistently and persistently watch and learn from Diamond distributors and do what they do. There are *No Limits* to what you can do, have or become. Study success.

96. Handle *Success:*

Keep your common sense and be gracious. If you see a person on the top of a mountain, they didn't just land there. Chances are they had to climb through many difficulties with a great expenditure of energy in order to get there. Diamonds work with a definite plan and an aim and a purpose in life and are envied by those less successful. Press on.

97. The major key to *Success*:

The key is to *work the business*. Success breeds success. Surround yourself with distributors who love what they are doing.

98. *Survival*:

- Bless and release people with ease.
- Do the best you can in a difficult situation.
- Give yourself credit for what you accomplish.
- Have patience with your distributors as they are figuring out their goals.
- Help others without expecting people to give back to you.
- Listen to those who need to be listened to.
- Reach out to encourage others.
- Remember that there are no statues erected to remember the critics.
- Stay positive while you navigate through tough times.
- When people are disloyal, unkind, and backstabbers, release them from your life immediately, have nothing more to do with them. Forgive them, and move on, building your future.
- When you are provoked, give yourself 24 hours before you react.

99. *Use the SWSWSW...NEXT...SW* formula:

Some will want to join you,
Some won't want to join you, so what?
Who are you going to ask next?
Someone is waiting!

100. The *Time* has come to Go Diamond:

The world has never been more ready for people to become leaders. The industry is waiting for you. Opportunity is everywhere. It certainly is about making money. It also offers alternatives to an 8-5 job and putting children in daycare. It allows you to pay off credit card debt, travel, get recognition, have a place to belong, and so much more. Now is **THE** time to *Go Diamond.*

101. Be *Trainable*:

Diamonds are teachable, coachable, trainable and always open to new ideas. Their attitude is: *"OK...teach me, coach me, train me...I want to learn this...I am the student. I want this information; I desire to learn how to get to the top. Tell me, give me the words, and show me what to do; I am ready, I am a sponge, ready to soak up the information. I am listening with all my heart; I am ready to take massive action now! I won't stop until I get to the top. I will stay coachable, for as long as it takes."*

102. *Teamwork* Gems:

When a highly motivated successline pulls together and when a successline unites, it becomes far more powerful than any individual. By working together using *The Go Diamond System*, developing leaders; success is inevitable. Develop team spirit and provide a place where people can belong and flourish. Teach everyone how to plug into *"The Go Diamond System,"* and as they achieve be sure to give them lots of recognition and encouragement. Develop the team attitude that *"Together, Everyone Achieves More."*

103. Be *Unselfish:*

Build leaders and make *THEM* successful.

104. Have a clear *Vision* of where you are going:

Have the vision of achieving the top position. Have a burning desire, a vision to get to the top, and navigate around all obstacles, and you will *Go Diamond*. Nothing and no situation will stop you. Being able to see yourself *Going Diamond* will give you that extra motivation and inspiration to continue on and on and on through tough times and good times. Have a vision of *Going Diamond* in a certain amount of time. What will it feel like? What will it look like? What will be the benefits to you of becoming a Diamond? Think all of this through. See it, believe it, and achieve it. Have *"Tunnel Vision."* Set your sights on *Going Diamond* and keep your eyes on this goal until you reach it. Avoid the many other good and fun things that can easily distract you from *Going Diamond*; put on your blinders. Avoid the temptations that come along all day long to take your focus off building your business. When you love what you do and have the vision of where you are going, what could be more fun than working towards that goal? Not much.

105. Have pure *Zeal*:

Prepare to pursue your goals with complete commitment. Unless you are unequivocally committed to a goal, don't even go there. Your purpose must be to go for greatness and it must be inseparable from your commitment to achieving your goal.

The traffic light system in the world is not complicated.

Keep it simple.

You are motivated to the degree that the decisions you make are **your** decisions. To **want** to *Go Diamond* is the key to motivation. You are always in a position to decide. You can decide to *Go Diamond* and you can decide not to *Go Diamond*. The choice is yours.

 Diamond Tip: Believe in your opportunity as if it is a ticket to financial freedom, as if your life depends upon it, because it does.

Chapter 5
Network Marketing, You've Got to Love it!
by Jan Ruhe

It was more than two decades ago that I was introduced to this industry. I was invited to a skin care party at a neighbor's home. I loved the idea of having a home party. I liked the concept of working from home. At the time I had a baby girl, Sarah who was about one year old and I was looking for something to do at home to make some extra money.

I was 27 years old and clueless about how to sell, how to recruit, and how to teach or train others how to do the business. I attended a complicated training and was discouraged as it seemed too hard to do the business.

Shortly after the training, I found out that I was expecting baby number two, son Clayton. We had a nice home but we were house poor. We didn't have any money left over for fine furnishings, nice clothes, travel or anything else. I wanted more. I began to take a risk and told people about the skin care line I was excited about. No one would buy from me. I could not persuade anyone to use the products. I loved them, but could not convince anyone else to use them. So I gave up and quit. In the back of my mind, I was hoping someone would recruit me into another company, but alas, no one did, for a long long time. My point? There are people looking. I was. I was ripe to be recruited and no one ever attempted for many years, no one even thought to ask me. A young mother with two little children, she must be too busy. I wasn't. I was a very organized person, I had loads of time. I spent hours with my children, and loved every minute of it. That did not change even when I did join for the second and last time. They were my pride and joy, they were my reason for getting up in the morning and I loved every precious second of being a mother.

Years later, I was invited to a home party and could not wait to attend. I joined another company in March of 1980 (the whole story is in my book <u>MLM Nuts $ Bolts</u>) and made a promise to myself that I would succeed. I loved the products and I wanted to make money selling them from my home. I was not going to quit this time. I had never been so enthusiastic about anything before in my entire life. From the day I put pen to paper I knew that I had found what I wanted to do for my life's career, Network Marketing. It promised a better future for my children. I was willing to work to get that lifestyle. I was willing to work it **big time**.

It wasn't the company or their mission statement that excited me. It was the products and the possibility that I could make money and make my children proud of me that floated my boat. By this time, baby number three, Ashley, was on the way. It wasn't that I was bored or unfulfilled or unhappy. Actually, even with a lot of personal drama going on, I was a very happy young woman, especially when I was with my children. Here is what got me excited, really *fired up*: for the first time in my life: I'd been shown a product that I could believe in and share with others that would sell easily. Educational toys, books, table top games and todays software. I could make some extra money and stay home and be a mommy. I still did not understand recruiting until several months later. When I did learn how to recruit and massively enroll or sponsor others I was unstoppable. I was in high gear and could not wait to get started. My raw enthusiasm was spilling over. Here was a way that my success in life could be directly proportionate to the level of service and support I provided for other people.

I went to work on me. I had discovered my life's passion. An opportunity that would allow me to become the very best person I could possibly be and make a positive difference with other people. I knew that this was what I would do for the rest of my life. And now, after two decades, I have been true to those early promises I made myself.

When I joined we had little money. Times were tough. We didn't have answering machines, PC's, laptops, fax machines, Mail Boxes, Etc., palm pilots, cell phones and email was unheard of. But I was willing to build a big business and wanted to participate in building the company nationwide. I believed that Network Marketing was such a unique and extraordinary system, where people could succeed beyond their wildest expectations, and much faster than I did. Once you grasp the unlimited potential of the opportunity, you will reveal your deepest desires and aspirations.

I heard about some people at the time who were making a lot of money selling products out of their home. For the first few years, I truly did not think it would pay off for me. I wasn't good enough; I wasn't like the heavy hitters in other companies; how could just a little housewife succeed, and with three little children no less. I didn't quit and would not give up even when I was discouraged. My point? Do not ever give up, give in, or give way to defeat. You must never, ever give up.

I began to read books and book-by-book, seminar by seminar, tape by tape I got courage, the words to say, patience and stickability. I studied leadership skills and champions. I checked out books from the library on how people got to the top. I was on fire with desire, and I believed in me. No one else did. I did though, and that's all that mattered. I would read a book, gather a group of people together and give a book report to them outloud. Why? Because I wanted to retain what I read. My point? If you teach something, your chances of retaining the material is better.

Then I found Jim Rohn, my mentor. He taught me success philosophies; to be the best and ignore the critics.

I had desire and drive and vision. You have these too, or you would not have chosen this book, *Go Diamond*! Just decide to decide to put your true desire and drive to work. It starts today.

I began to have a vision, a dream and massive desire of a fantastic future and played a *"What if?"* game. What if I worked really hard at this for five years? Could I get a big home? Could I drive a sports car? Could I college educate my children? Have beautiful clothes and jewels? Invest in great interior home furnishings? Travel the world? Have a network of friends around the world? I began to make a Master Dream list. I wrote down everything I could ever imagine getting, that I wanted even in my deepest secrets. Things I had never dreamed I could dream. And I asked myself the questions. *Why not me? Why not now?* Why wait on anyone to make me successful. What if I worked hard for 10 years, what would my life look like then? I dared not dream 20 years into the future, I just couldn't. Not then.

I had always, always, always wanted and expected a man to financially support me. My father was a fantastic provider and my mother was a wonderful stay at home mother. Why couldn't I be like that too? I didn't like asking my husband at the time for $10 and him questioning me on what I wanted it for. He also liked the words *practical* and *budget*. I hated those words and that mentality was brutal for me to live with. I hated the words *"we can't afford it."* So, I set some goals, big goals, and began to go to work on perfecting all of the *Go Diamond* gems in this book. I went to work on changing me. Big time. One by one, I began to achieve my goals. All of them. I would not be denied.

I was willing to work to achieve the Diamond level and did not stop until I got there.

Today I don't recruit direct to me anymore. I am so thankful that I'm the top earning Diamond in my company (for many years) and am also an accomplished author of many books sold in several languages worldwide. I am also a worldwide Master Trainer. These accomplishments amaze and humble me. I really only wanted to stay at home and raise my children while making some extra money. Along the way, I persevered, had unkind critics try to stop my path to Diamond, and went through a long messy divorce. Today I am married to my best friend, Bill Ruhe, and my three children have turned out to all be champion young adults. I have no regrets, not one.

Network Marketing is one of the true gifts of our time. Fall in love with Network Marketing like love at first sight. Love and cherish it.

My mission today in life is to let people know that they CAN *Go Diamond*. I can show you how to do the business too, and shave at least three years off your learning curve. I am a passionate teacher.

Bill and I have loved traveling the world together sharing our wisdom, normally 11-12 countries a year. We look forward to seeing you at our events and know that with this book, you can go faster than ever before to *Going Diamond*. Prepare yourself for a life of abundance and prosperity. After using *The Go Diamond System* you will be a more effective Networker, you will strengthen your successline, and you will boost your team's momentum.

Living the lifestyle has been fabulous. We have had many fantastic trips around the world. We have flown to South Africa and have been the guest at a private game ranch, visited Botswana and Zimbabwe. We have been to Seoul, South Korea. We have walked hand in hand on the beaches in Jeju Island, South Korea; in Capetown and Knysna, South Africa; Southern France, Monaco, Spain, Morocco, Mexico, the Bahamas; the Caribbean and in Hawaii. We have been to Hong Kong, China, Austria, Switzerland, Spain, Botswana, Zimbabwe, Morocco, Mexico, Canada, the UK, Ireland, Scotland, Italy, and across the USA. It's been an amazing treat to live this lifestyle and have the friends worldwide that we have. Three of my favorite trips were:

1. To celebrate Bill's sixtieth birthday. We went on the famous Orient Express from London all the way to Rome, through the Alps and rested and relaxed and spent time together.

2. Taking my daughters on a mother/daughter safari to Kenya, Africa.

3. Taking the Rovos Rail from Johannesburg, South Africa to Capetown, South Africa, across the lower Karoo to the Cape of Good Hope.

I have to pinch myself that we get to experience the lifestyle that becoming a Diamond in Network Marketing brought me. It will for you too. Believe it, achieve it….press on my friends….persist until you succeed. You can have it all, success is waiting for you on a silver platter, come to the table of plenty.

Here is the route the Orient Express took us:

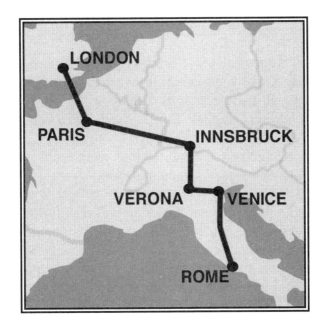

Live the Diamond Lifestyle
Fire Up!
Don't be Average, Be a Champion.
Have the Rhino Spirit
and be unstoppable.

Knowing *No Limits!*

by Jayne Leach

Nine years ago, I was not a *No Limits* person. I had just gone through a nasty divorce, lost my home and income as they both went with my now ex-husband. My husband's last words to me were *"I have no respect for you and you will never amount to anything without me."* Hurtful words, and devastating for me at the time. Looking back, I can say that they were the words that motivated me to go on and achieve greatness in my life, way beyond my wildest dreams at that time.

We had enjoyed a wonderful life. My husband was a farm manager for a large estate. We had a lovely old farmhouse, nice cars on the farm, horses in the field and above all two great sons. I thought we had it made. Then I found out that my husband was unfaithful to me. It was a sickening blow and during the two years that followed, I stayed with him for the sake of the boys. I thought we could perhaps make things work but it was not to be; I was wasting my life and wanted something more.

On a wet, miserable day, with no money and no idea how I was going to cope, I packed two suitcases and left with my sons. Our home for 18 months was a rented farm cottage. It was small, damp and in very bad order. It had leaking windows when it rained and heating didn't work properly and the landlord had a nightmare personality to deal with. My husband could not believe I would leave him and made life as unbearable as possible. This was a difficult time for the boys and me but we were strong for each other and managed to get through the first few months of our new life together. I had long lonely nights in my little house, thinking about my future and what was to become of us. I had no money and no job prospects but I also needed to put food on the table and pay for our wretched cottage, so I managed to find some occasional and very poorly paid part time work from local farmers. If I wanted to give my boys the very best in life, something had to change, but what could? My background was in farming and horses and that was all I was qualified to do, but there was no way I could work in those fields and earn enough money to educate my sons privately and have all the good things in life. Where was I going to go? I really felt lost in a vicious circle where I was stuck in the middle. No qualifications, no job; no job, no money; no money, no future. Then the landlord increased the rent. Not having any means by which to raise the extra money, my landlord said I had 4 months left before the rent increased and then I would be out.

This was the worst point in my life. I was slowly sinking. Looking back now, it was a turning point, the time when I really had to face the future and I realized that if something didn't change, then I did not know what would become of us. When you hit a time like this in life, you have to take full responsibility and make some difficult choices. You cannot expect others to bail you out, if you want your life to change. Doors start opening and people start coming into your life; maybe they were always there, but we just hadn't seen them before.

Two things happened that changed me. First, I was invited to a wedding reception, but I felt so low that it was not something I wanted to attend. After telling my friend that I wasn't going, another invitation came for me to go to dinner with some friends in the village. Their son went to school with mine, so I decided to go. I was not into the social scene at that point. I was still hurting too much from my past. I turned up late and all the guests were talking and in couples, except one guy. He sat in the corner of the room, looking as sad and lonely as I felt. We were introduced and started chatting. He shared that he had just split up with his wife and had two children to look after, as well was running the UK part of a multi-national company. He was hurting as much as I was, so we spent the rest of the evening feeling a little sorry for ourselves as a result of our personal situations. That one meeting is where I met John Curtis. At the end of that evening, John said, *"You know, when you find something to get your teeth into, you will be a star; you have a lovely personality and you are clearly destined for great things!"* I was lost for words and emotional at the same time. Someone was saying nice things to me and I was lost for words. Someone thought I was worthy of greater things in my life.

I left that diner party feeling wonderful, for the first time in a long time. I believed in me after that night.

I went to a local shopping center later that same week. There was a big career opportunity exhibition taking place. I walked around and saw a stand with lots of people milling about, so I went closer and a young man came up to speak to me. He introduced himself and as the conversation developed, he explained they were recruiting right now and asked if I would be interested in having some information. You bet I was interested but then I felt I had to tell him that I had no experience whatsoever in marketing and selling; I was just a farmer and a mum. He said *"Great! It doesn't matter!"* then gave me some leaflets and took my number for a follow up call.

The call came and the distributor asked if he could come to show me the detail about how his company worked and what I could expect to get, if I became involved. The day that he was to come, I was so excited about the possibilities and I was not to be disappointed. He showed me a way to earn money by building a team of distributors and then began to draw circles and then more circles; and with those circles, suddenly I saw a way to educate my boys; get back my lifestyle; to have the nice things in life; and to build a massive business that was to be mine, which no one could take away from me; total security. I had no idea how to do it or if it would even work for me; but the concept of Network Marketing just grabbed my imagination and I was hooked.

I joined that company and for a few weeks went to the trainings and meetings. I heard a lot of people talk about life-changing experiences, but soon I realized that it wasn't quite right for me. Then another turn happened in my life. A friend of mine called excited about a company she had found. Another Network Marketing opportunity. Well, if she was in it, I had better have a look. I did and joined and had a ball, climbing up the compensation plan and making some decent money. John was becoming interested in joining me in the business, so we made some big plans. Then one evening, we got a call saying that the company had closed it's operation. All my dreams were dashed again. The vision I had for Matthew and Marcus going to private school were gone, and I was back to square one. This Network Marketing was not what I had hoped it would be, so I started looking for a job again and life was grim.

We got a phone call from someone we had met just briefly in another company and our lives changed for the better, forever. He was very excited about an American company who had just arrived in the UK, that was big, cash rich, debt free, opening up all over the world and with an amazing range of products. I was now skeptical but I still had big dreams and anyway, how was I going to achieve them in a job? So, John and I went to look. It was all we had dreamed of in a company. They had a great plan, fantastic products, sound management, a fantastic track record and people making huge amounts of money in countries where they had been open for a while. My gut feeling was to run with this and run with it I did. I grabbed it with both hands and worked so very hard. It has never let me down in the years since.

I am now a *No Limits* person, are you?

I went from rock bottom, to being totally financially secure. I went from renting a seedy little house, to having a 55 acre country estate and beautiful home; from driving an old rusty car, to having several Mercedes and other cars; from taking my boys to poor quality schools to top private schools; from no vacations to traveling the world and staying at 5 star properties; from less than £60 ($100) in the bank to having earned close to £2 million ($3 million)! From having no self-esteem to being passionate about what I do, able to speak in front of thousands of people all over the world.

Here is how I did it: I decided to! I was not going to waste my life worrying about the past. The future is what counts and time is very precious so don't waste it. Decide what kind of life you want and go for it. Seek out the people and opportunities that will do it for you. Network Marketing is the best way in the world to give you the chance to have, be and do whatever you want.

I refused to let anyone steal my dreams, even though on many occasions people tried. We all have dreams in our lives and the sad part is that most people lose sight of them and eventually let them slip away, believing that they will never achieve them. All of us have the right to a good life and to peace of mind. Don't settle for second best. Develop the mindset *"Failure is not an option"* and determine to achieve, come what may. Do not be denied. If you think like that and are prepared to open your mind to developing that thought process, then all of your dreams will come your way and you will be a *No Limits* person.

I went back to school. There is no way to learn Network Marketing in a day. I wanted to learn badly enough, and I learned fast. When you learn fast, you can achieve fast. I had to reach the Diamond position as fast as possible and to do that I had to learn the system and about the industry. Feed your mind by reading books like this one. I never missed a meeting or training and encouraged my successline to do the same. My view was that if I went to a meeting and someone shared just one idea that could change my way of thinking, I could achieve my goals faster. And it was time well spent. We must be serious students of this industry.

I became a leader. As more and more distributors joined my team, they were looking to me for support and inspiration. I couldn't let them down. I wanted to become a great leader. My business depended on me learning some leadership skill and so will yours. I learned to be a person who could inspire and motivate; a person who could teach and train others how to work the system fast and effectively; a person who helped people in my successline reach positions fast. I was a person doing the business, not just talking about it. So, my advice? Learn leadership as fast as you can. Here is a great definition: a leader is someone who is willing to do what others aren't willing to do, in order to enjoy the lifestyle that others don't and won't have.

I became self motivated. So many people rely on others to motivate them all the time. My mantra was: *"If it's going to be, it's up to me."* There were times when I needed a boost from my upline, but I never moaned to him. I just got on with it.

I worked on my attitude. Do you? You can teach a person all the skill in the world; but if they have a lousy attitude, it's all a waste of time. A positive attitude is your passport to a better future. Stay away from negative, hurtful people. Hang out with successful distributors and leaders and never ever take advice or attend a seminar by someone who hasn't achieved what you want.

I eradicated the word *"failure"* from my vocabulary and injected a real sense of urgency into my business. I couldn't afford to hang around; I wanted success. I wanted it now and I was prepared to take action, to do whatever it took. I learned the system, became a leader, focused on my goals, helped others, changed my attitude and success came my way. It can come your way too. Networking with the right company will never let you down. The only people who fail in our industry are the ones that quit, losing their focus and giving up. It is such a shame. When you stick with it, you can have anything you want.

Do you have dreams not yet realized? Do you want more out of life? This book will really help you focus on how to build a massive organization. Read it once, then read it again and go out and Network as if your life depends on it, because truly, it does.

> There are *No Limits* to our possibilities. At any moment, we have more possibilities than we can act upon. When we imagine the possibilities, our vision expands, we capture our dreams and our life is full.

 Diamond Tip: Failure is not an option.

Acres of Diamonds

There once lived not far from the River Indus, an ancient Persian by the name of Al Hafed. It was said that Al Hafed owned a very large farm with orchards, grain fields and gardens. He was a contented and wealthy man — contented because he was wealthy, and wealthy because he was contented. One day there visited this old farmer, one of those ancient Buddhist priests, and he sat down by Al Hafed's fire and told that old farmer how this world of ours was made.

He said that this world was once a mere bank of fog, which is scientifically true, and he said that the Almighty thrust his finger into the bank of fog and then began slowly to move his finger around and gradually to increase the speed of his finger until at last he whirled that bank of fog into a solid ball of fire, and it went rolling through the universe, burning its way through other cosmic banks of fog, until it condensed the moisture without, and fell in floods of rain upon the heated surface and cooled the outward crust. Then the internal flames burst through the cooling crust and threw up the mountains and made the hills and the valleys of this wonderful world of ours. If this internal melted mass burst out and cooled very quickly it became granite; that which cooled less quickly became silver; and less quickly, gold; and after gold diamonds were made. Said the old priest, *"A Diamond is a congealed drop of sunlight."*

This is a scientific truth also. You all know that a Diamond is pure carbon, actually deposited sunlight — and he said another thing I would not forget: he declared that a Diamond is the last and highest of God's mineral creations, as a woman is the last and highest of God's animal creations. I suppose that is the reason why the two have such a liking for each other. And the old priest told Al Hafed that if he had a handful of Diamonds he could purchase a whole country, and with a mine of Diamonds he could place his children upon thrones through the influence of their great wealth.

Al Hafed heard all about Diamonds and how much they were worth, and went to his bed that night a poor man — not that he had lost anything, but poor because he was discontented and discontented because he thought he was poor. He said: *"I want a mine of Diamonds!"* So he lay awake all night, and early in the morning sought out the priest.

Now I know from experience that a priest when awakened early in the morning is cross. He awoke that priest out of his dreams and said to him, *"Will you tell me where I can find Diamonds?"* The priest said, *"Diamonds? What do you want with Diamonds?"* *"I want to be immensely rich,"* said Al Hafed, *"but I don't know where to go."* *"Well,"* said the priest, *"if you will find a river that runs over white sand between high mountains, in those sands you will always see Diamonds."* *"Do you really believe that there is such a river?"* *"Plenty of them, plenty of them; all you have to do is just go and find them, then you have them."* Al Hafed said, *"I will go."* So he sold his farm, collected his money and interest, left his family in the charge of a neighbor, and away he went in search of Diamonds.

He began very properly, to my mind, at the Mountains of the Moon. Afterwards he went around into Palestine, then wandered on into Europe, and at last, when his money was all spent, and he was in rags, wretchedness and poverty, he stood on the shore of that bay in Barcelona, Spain, when a tidal wave came rolling in through the Pillars of Hercules and the poor, afflicted, suffering man could not resist the awful temptation to cast himself into that incoming tide, and he sank beneath its foaming crest, never to rise in this life again.

When that old guide had told me that very sad story, he stopped the camel I was riding and went back to fix the baggage on one of the other camels, and I remember thinking to myself, *"Why did he reserve that for his particular friends?"* There seemed to be no beginning, middle or end — nothing to it.

When the guide came back and took up the halter of my camel again, he went right on with the same story. He said that Al Hafed's successor led his camel out into the garden to drink, and as that camel put its nose down into the clear water of the garden brook, Al Hafed's successor noticed a curious flash of light from the sands of the shallow stream, and reaching in he pulled out a black stone having an eye of light that reflected all the colors of the rainbow, and he took that curious pebble into the house and left it on the mantel, then went on his way and forgot all about it.

A few days after that, this same old priest who told Al Hafed how Diamonds were made, came in to visit his successor, when he saw that flash of light from the mantel. He rushed up and said, *"Here is a Diamond — here is a Diamond! Has Al Hafed returned?"* *"No, no; Al Hafed has not returned and that is not a Diamond; that is nothing but a stone; we found it right out here in our garden."* *"But I know a Diamond when I see it,"* said he; *"that is a Diamond!"*

Then together they rushed to the garden and stirred up the white sands with their fingers and found others more beautiful and valuable than the first. That is when the Diamond mines of Golconda, the most magnificent diamond mines in all the history of mankind, exceeding the Kimberley in its value, were discovered. The great Kohinoor Diamond in England's crown jewels and the largest crown diamond on earth in Russia's crown jewels, which I had often hoped she would have to sell before they had peace with Japan, came from that mine, and when the old guide had called my attention to that wonderful discovery, he took his Turkish cap off his head again and swung it around in the air to call my attention to the moral.

The moral of the story is this: if Al Hafed had remained at home and dug in his own cellar or in his own garden, instead of wretchedness, starvation, poverty and death in a strange land, he would have had *"acres of diamonds"*. For every acre, yes, every shovelful of that old farm afterwards revealed the gems which since have decorated the crowns of monarchs.

> *The Diamond title is not limited.*
>
> *It's for anyone who has exquisite taste*
>
> *and an understanding and appreciation*
>
> *for the finer things in life.*

 Diamond Tip: Get busy. Your future starts today! Fortune favors the brave.

The Daffodil Principle

Several times my daughter had telephoned to say, *"Mother, you must come see the daffodils before they are over."* I wanted to go, but it was a two-hour drive from Laguna to Lake Arrowhead. *"I will come next Tuesday,"* I promised, a little reluctantly, on her third call. Next Tuesday dawned cold and rainy. Still, I had promised, and so I drove there. When I finally walked into Carolyn's house and hugged and greeted my grandchildren, I said, *"Forget the daffodils, Carolyn! The road is invisible in the clouds and fog, and there is nothing in the world except you and these children that I want to see bad enough to drive another inch!"* My daughter smiled calmly and said, *"We drive in this all the time, Mother."* *"Well, you won't get me back on the road until it clears, and then I'm heading for home!"* I assured her. *"I was hoping you'd take me over to the garage to pick up my car."* *"How far will we have to drive?"* I asked. *"Just a few blocks,"* Carolyn said. *"I'll drive. I'm used to this."* After several minutes, I had to ask, *"Where are we going? This isn't the way to the garage!"* *"We're going to my garage the long way,"* Carolyn smiled, *"by way of the daffodils."* *"Carolyn,"* I said sternly, *"please turn around."* *"It's all right, Mother, I promise. You will never forgive yourself if you miss this experience."*

After about twenty minutes, we turned onto a small gravel road and I saw a small church. On the far side of the church, I saw a hand-lettered sign that read, *"Daffodil Garden."* We got out of the car and each took a child's hand, and I followed Carolyn down the path. Then, we turned a corner of the path, and I looked up and gasped. Before me lay the most glorious sight. It looked as though someone had taken a great vat of gold and poured it down over the mountain peak and slopes. The flowers were planted in majestic, swirling patterns — great ribbons and swaths of deep orange, white, lemon yellow, salmon pink, saffron, and butter yellow. Each different-colored variety was planted as a group so that it swirled and flowed like its own river with its own unique hue. There were five acres of flowers.

"But who has done this?" I asked Carolyn. *"It's just one woman,"* Carolyn answered. *"She lives on the property. That's her home."* Carolyn pointed to

a well-kept A-frame house that looked small and modest in the midst of all that glory. We walked up to the house. On the patio, we saw a poster. *"Answers to the Questions I Know You Are Asking"* was the headline. The first answer was a simple one: *"50,000 bulbs,"* it read. The second answer was, *"one at a time, by one woman. Two hands, two feet, and very little brain."* The third answer was, *"Began in 1958."* There it was. **The Daffodil Principle.** For me, that moment was a life-changing experience. I thought of this woman whom I had never met, who, more than thirty-five years before, had begun — one bulb at a time — to bring her vision of beauty and joy to an obscure mountaintop. Still, just planting one bulb at a time, year after year, had changed the world. This unknown woman had forever changed the world in which she lived. She had created something of ineffable magnificence, beauty, and inspiration. The principle her daffodil garden taught is one of the greatest principles of celebration. That is, learning to move toward our goals and desires one step at a time — often just one baby-step at a time — and learning to love the doing, learning to use the accumulation of time. When we multiply tiny pieces of time with small increments of daily effort, we too will find we can accomplish magnificent things. We can change the world. *"It makes me sad in a way,"* I admitted to Carolyn. *"What might I have accomplished if I had thought of a wonderful goal thirty-five years ago and had worked away at it 'one bulb at a time' through all those years? Just think what I might have been able to achieve!"* My daughter summed up the message of the day in her direct way.

"Start tomorrow," she said. It's so pointless to think of the lost hours of yesterdays. The way to make learning a lesson a celebration instead of a cause for regret, is to only ask, *"How can I put this to use today?"*

 Diamond Tip: It all starts with finding one person to join you and teaching them to do the same.

How to *Go Diamond* in the Fast Lane

When a distributor gets to Diamond and is asked the secret of their success, usually that person answers *"Hard Work!"* Well, what does that tell everyone else? What does that really mean? We normally start wondering what the *real secret* is behind their good fortune.

Was it a lucky break? Did they start out with lots of people joining them from another company? The fact they have a big name in the industry? They married into a successline at the top? They got the successline in a divorce? Someone very wealthy set them up or whatever it could be that made them so successful? Questions like this might comfort our own sagging ego but they also blind us to the truth. The truth, in most cases, is that when Diamonds say they accomplished their objectives with hard work, *they mean it!*

Many distributors work hard too, don't they? And yet they aren't at the Diamond level. Most distributors' definition of hard work is probably less than 40 hours a week of their best effort, with dinners at home and weekends spent in fun and relaxation.

When Diamonds use the term *"hard work,"* they mean working at top capacity, often 70-80 hours a week, every week; loving their work until it becomes their driving passion and they devote all their waking hours to thinking, planning and striving toward their goals, which others consider impossible. It's called….. Total Commitment.

Total commitment is not a recommended life-style for everyone. For most distributors, the price it extracts is much too much, but there are also countless thousands who know exactly what they want and are willing to give as much of themselves as necessary in order to *Go Diamond.*

Are you willing to work hard to *Go Diamond?* To go all out? To sacrifice certain pleasures because your time and energy must be devoted to this massive goal? Will you be happy to make these sacrifices?

If your answer is *"yes!"* you want to *Go Diamond*, then you are right on target. You have found the right goal for the inner you. However, if you think you will begrudge giving up evenings to work and resent sometimes having to pass up weekend fun, then think again. You may not want to *Go Diamond*, just partway. Your true goal probably lies elsewhere.

Distributors who *Go Diamond* have the single-minded devotion to *Go Diamond,* that is best described as total commitment. Some people refer to Diamonds as workaholics. But that implies illness, and if you are doing what you want to do more than anything else in the world, why should you punish yourself by cutting down on the things that make you happy?

Going Diamond does not necessarily preclude a happy marriage, but those distributors who want to *Go Diamond*, who play for the highest stakes, often find that their total commitment means that their spouse better be right in there helping and being a part of achieving this goal. The pivotal quality that Diamonds have is total commitment, the ability and desire to work to top capacity. They find their work exciting and rewarding as they seek the Diamond level. Total commitment is the common denominator among successful distributors. Its importance cannot be underestimated. You cannot kid yourself. You must burn all bridges behind you, so that there is no escape route to turn back. You must be willing to put every ounce of energy into your work right from the day you make the decision.

Diamonds must have good health and boundless energy. *Going Diamond* demands strength. Distributors are born with differing energy reserves. The distributor who tires fast, burns out easily, would do well to reset his or her goals. There are many distributors content with a smaller degree of success and their goals are honorable and satisfying to them. They are the ones who take a lot of time to read, go to the theater, are the scout leaders, the Sunday School teachers; they are the parents who go on the field trips, who are the Home Room Mothers, the ones who hang out at the pool, spend a lot of time visiting their families, watch TV a lot, indulge in the joys of friendship, so that they can nurture human values. But the Diamonds who have ambition, who want to soar to the top, do not see their total commitment as a sacrifice. To their way of thinking, they are gaining. They feel totally fulfilled and happy. And they find quality time to spend with friends and family. They love hanging out with others who have gotten to the top level.

They can work for days with little sleep because they are caught up with details of producing a huge successline. Once in a while, when everything is just right, there's a moment of magic. Diamonds can live on moments of magic. Diamonds who are totally committed to being the best they can be, refer to it as a peak state; that is a peak experience that is a very strong argument for not resisting the seduction of total commitment.

To most distributors, total commitment is a sign of misplaced values, or even disease. Diamonds love what they do, they want to do what they do and love every minute of it. Diamonds are a breed apart. They are strivers. They are always reaching, higher than most distributors, and higher than the last time they tried. The rewards of their drive are staggering: Money, Influence, Power, Prestige, and the joys of their commitment.

Success follows actions that seem to need no conscious intervention on the part of the distributor *Going Diamond*. There is no hurry, there are no distracting demands on attention. Moment flows into moment. Past and future disappear. So does the distinction between oneself and the activity to *Go Diamond*.

Why do some people play so hard? What make distributors decide to go Diamond and give their all? Is it the prestige? The glamour? The prospect of winning? Well, what it is, is that the chief attraction to *Going Diamond* is the altered state of being, the identity, making a difference, and proving to yourself that you can do it. Diamonds have an ability to concentrate remarkably. They feel very much in control of themselves and their world. The first requirement is to work as hard as you can at something that presents a challenge. Not even the Diamond challenge, but something that stretches you just a little, then makes you realize that you are doing something better today than you did yesterday or the last time you attempted to do it. You must have a significant span of uninterrupted time. It's virtually impossible to *Go Diamond* if you are interrupted every few minutes.

No one can or should remain in constant commitment to *Going Diamond*. That would be too draining. It can be stressful but it is a healthy stress. Successful people are healthier than those who are unsuccessful or only trying to be successful. Stress is a positive factor in health. Diamonds enjoy the stress of coping with challenges. They are attracted to what we refer to as: *"the call of controlled risk."* They seek it because they are full of energy. They feel more vital when they are active. Your body's system is self-protective. You will not be able to switch yourself into a fired up state often enough, to cause you harm or unhealthy stress.

Total commitment is not just hard work; it is total involvement. Building a rock wall is backbreaking work. There are some people who build rock walls all their lives. They worked hard. But there are other people who build rock walls and all the time that they are placing one rock on top of another, they have a vision in their minds, a goal. When they finish the wall, they have more than just a wall. It's the goal that makes the difference.

If you know what it is you want out of life and you are totally committed to working for it, then all sorts of opportunities open up. Many of them will open up for you because of inertia. Other people's inertia, not yours. Most people are basically lazy. Even the people who are blessed with boundless energy and a burning fire of desire. The secret is to understand this and promise yourself that you will not give in to your laziness. Search for ways to do your business better, so you can be more productive. This is important for you on your path to *Going Diamond*. You cannot become lazy. The distributor who succeeds fastest is the one who does the *"too much"* and who builds the most leaders and who makes them successful.

The moral is: think of total commitment as the only way of life that will result in your attaining your goal of being a fabulously successful Diamond. You will find that the sacrifices are insignificant, in view of the fact that you are doing just what you want to do most. So when it comes to the seduction to total commitment to get yourself to *Go Diamond*, yield.

When you have made the commitment and are determined to *Go Diamond*, it's amazing how life will rearrange itself to accommodate you to reach that goal. It's called taking yourself to the next level and then the next level and on up the compensation plan to the top, and not stopping until you get there.

Once you make the decision, no matter where you are in the circle of your life, prepare for explosive growth. When you go into action, you will produce results. Activity breeds productivity. And you will begin to stack your successes upon your successes. When you go into action, that causes commotion; when you are in commotion, that breeds promotion. Our advice? Go into massive action!

 Diamond Tip: The greatest glory is not in never failing, but in rising every time we fall. Get totally committed to *Going Diamond* and don't look back until you get there.

Feed your Mind

Readers are leaders and leaders are readers. No doubt about it. It's the distributor who can say that after studying, *"What a wealth of wisdom!"*

You have before you a splendid opportunity to *Go Diamond,* but always remember that nothing but work and brains count. No fairy godmother will help you succeed. You have to wave your own magic wand over your situation and go to work on yourself. For financial success to occur, personal growth and development must occur.

You can only *Go Diamond* by your own sense of direction and relentless work. There is no substitute for work. If you are work-shy, you will not achieve the Diamond level. Your life is a precious jewel and no one ever defined its true value better than Ralph Waldo Emerson. He said you must *"pay the price"* for your actions, good or bad. Once you accept the fact, and many cannot, that there is a Law of Compensation which governs all your thoughts and deeds; you will have uncovered the secret of directing your life in any direction you choose.

The Law of Compensation has never been repealed. You have to live with it, whether you like it or not, so you might as well use it to your advantage. We promise you, you will be happy if you do.

When your present approach is not getting you to Diamond, it's time to take different actions. Not many distributors get a blinding flash of insight that says: *"What you are doing so far is not working. Here is the path to take from here on."* The knowledge that our career is not going where we expect it to, usually steals up on us gradually. We feel somewhat dissatisfied, without knowing or understanding why. We aren't having fun with what we are doing and don't see clearly where we are going.

That's when you know it's time to change. Change does not emerge full-blown in your mind. You have to prepare yourself to begin to be a student, to start to do things differently, to decide on different goals and replace losing habits with winning ones.

Here is how to start to change what you are thinking about, reading, believing and to start on the new path to *Going Diamond*:

Be careful who you listen to:
Listen to those living the lifestyle you desire and those who get massive results. Keep yourself in a positive shell, don't let any negative thoughts inside of it. Write your own recipe for success.

Brain Stimulators:
Can I suffer from going for greatness?
Can I utilize my time, efforts and energies to *Go Diamond* faster?
What am I trying to accomplish?
Why do I think what I want to do is possible?
What causes me to think it might be impossible?
What do I stand to gain, or to lose?
Will factors such as my age, stamina or health have any bearing on the outcome?
What does going for greatness mean to me?

Chill out:
Take time to live. We do not primarily live to work. We work to live.

Come from Contribution:
Want to make a difference; want to help the success of the successline, to keep the flame of success shining brightly? Be the one who does care. Be the leader, *Go Diamond*! Be a go giver, as well as a go getter.

Create a Daily Routine:
Take a look at what you do daily. You are most likely doing the same things over and over, day after day. The average distributor is getting nowhere, on the one project that he or she needs to work on to get to the next level. Do what you need to do early in the day; don't cluster what you need to do at the end of the day.

Don't get too busy:
Isn't it interesting that people who tell us how busy they are, have the time to tell us how busy they are? Stop saying you are busy. No one cares. It doesn't make you more important; it makes you look like you are doing too much. Watch your words.

Don't miss seeing the amazing things on the earth:
Feed your mind by going to museums, The Vatican, seeing the Mona Lisa, traveling on the Orient Express, reading the great books, looking at paintings, listening to the music. Every night stretches over us the amazing canopy of the heavens. Bring yourself to a stop when you are

in the country and star gaze. This glory is for our inspiration nightly; don't be such in a hurry that you bypass it. The full moons, a fireplace ablaze, easy chairs to rest in, beautiful rugs on the floor. As we look about us on our planet, with its exquisite beauty and obvious delights, when you *Go Diamond,* take time to really enjoy the lifestyle. When you do, you have mastered the art of living. Learn a new language or at least some words to help you communicate in another language. See the world.

Do something Doable:

Some days the goal of *Going Diamond* is so far away, challenges are so great, your personal weaknesses seem so large. You end up in a losing rut. Many distributors think this is the time to sit back and review their whole life. That could be the very worst thing you can do. When you are discouraged, challenges appear insurmountable. Thinking about the entire dismal scene will just push you further down into the dumps. Instead, try AMAP, **A M**inimum **A**ccomplishment **P**lan. Pick out something you can do for sure. It doesn't have to be something huge. And do it. If you do, that one accomplishment can give you a lift and fuel the fires for more ambitious goals. If *Going Diamond* is too much for now, but you know it's for you, then take on some minor goals, and do the doable.

Embrace Change:

Do things differently. Talk less and think more. Ponder challenges in solitude. Change your routine. Shake up your pattern. Don't wait until you have a new strategy; change your way of doing things first.

For the Habit of Success:

If your actions do not answer a need, they do not need to be part of your day. Take action that satisfies a need. Habits always come from inside. We don't get rid of *"bad habits,"* we replace them. We acquire them in the same way that bad habits are acquired, and we work to change them. Change habits one at a time.

Get a sense of meaning:

Connect what you are doing with a purpose and worthy achievement. Want this:

- A chance to achieve, to build something and to recognize what you have accomplished.
- A title and identity that is yours.
- A connection with an organization that you can loyally serve.
- Honorable and good relations with the peers with whom you work.

Get into the habit of reading:

Just read something positive every day. Get into the habit of listening to tapes, to turning your car into a rolling classroom. Read biographies of people who have gotten amazing results. Study the top people in your company. Walk out of seminars taught by people who are not living the lifestyle you want to have. Listen to those who have what you want. Take copious notes and say to yourself that Life will NEVER be the same again after that book, CD, tape or seminar. Take action on what you learn. Go for greatness! Do not be average, be a champion!

It's never too late for you courageous distributors, to raise yourselves out of what you consider ruts and switch to entirely different goals, which will satisfy your innermost longings:

You possess an adequate freedom to make what you are able to make of yourself, your life, and your career. Those who make nothing, advance nowhere and simply exist, because they refuse to make the effort to have more or get better, are making a choice. Distributors who make an honest and forceful effort but who perhaps have shortcomings or physical infirmities, need our understanding, empathy and, where justified, a helping hand. Then there are the Diamonds, who achieve the status they work to achieve. While they are often aided in some measure by others, their successes are due in large part to their own talents, efforts and determination. Most distributors fail not because they try to do too much but because they fail to do enough.

Keep learning and growing:

We don't understand why some distributors *Go Diamond* and most don't. Prepare your mind and you have a better chance to *Go Diamond*. Don't let your talents go to waste. You can have individual fulfillment and lifelong learning.

Make new friends, but keep the old; one is Silver and the other Gold:

Cultivate new friends. Mark Twain reminded us that good books and good friends make the ideal life. Never overlook the chance to make a new friend. Cultivate the habit of looking for the interesting qualities and values in others. There is something very fascinating to learn in every single person you meet.

Never stop being the student:

Keep feeding your mind. Always be open to new ideas.

Start today:

You have but to stretch forward your hand and accept success. Have no fear of any sort or type. If you have skills, apply them. If you don't, attain them. The world needs to profit by you. Go forth and do that which is within you to do; take no heed of the critics. Do not ask for permission to succeed beyond your wildest expectations. Fortune waits upon every phone call, every footstep you take. Fortune belongs to you. Start now. Stretch out your hand and grasp prosperity. Life is an emergency. Cleanse your brain, strengthen your will. It will take possession of you. It waits upon you to decide. Start tonight; start now upon this new journey to *Going Diamond*.

Stop Starving Your Spirit:

Take time to live the lifestyle, you so richly deserve.

Take a Fresh Look at *Going Diamond*:

Begin with a clear focus on *Going Diamond*. How long has it been since you even thought about *Going Diamond*? Does *Going Diamond* still look as good as it did? At this time in your career, does *Going Diamond* seem like the right goal for you? How much progress have you made? Are you letting obstacles get in your way? Can they be overcome? Do you feel like making the effort to overcome them? Are you willing to struggle to *Go Diamond*? How long do you think it will take you to get there? Are you willing to get more committed to reaching the Diamond level?

Powerful Treasure Mapping and I-Cans

Your vision of the future starts by making your own treasure map. Here is how: Get some magazines, new and old, all kinds of magazines. Cut out pictures of what you desire in life and glue the photos on either a piece of paper, a large poster board or even on a postcard. Get the vision of what you are willing to work for.

During one of Jan's visits to the UK, Rob Forster, a top networker, showed her his old treasure maps, made over a decade ago. They showed a Rolex watch, a Rolls Royce, horses, helicopters and so much more. Today, Rob has earned enough money in Network Marketing to get everything that was on those early treasure maps. He even showed Jan a photo of a tree-lined lane he now drives his Rolls Royce down, in order to get to his estate. It's powerful to do a treasure map!

Before a Treasure Map Training say this:
- At our next meeting, please bring old and new magazines that you will share with the team.
- Also, bring scissors and glue sticks and the trainer will provide the poster board.
- Bring a large empty container.

Say this at your training:
- Today you have all brought magazines. Let's share them with everyone and start finding pictures of what your life is going to look like when you *Go Diamond*!
- It's time to shift your focus away from high concentrated effort of just selling products and booking more events, to including in your presentation sharing the opportunity to become a distributor. It's time to kick it up a notch and begin to massively recruit others into your business. If *Going Diamond* is what you have made your mind up to be, then it will happen. You will start to talk about the opportunity for

others more and more. Today, the time has come for you to think "*as if*" you are already a Diamond. As a Diamond, your job is to now recruit and train new distributors, people who want to do what you want to do. Now let's get into the magazines and create our vision of our future life.

Do this at a training:
- Have everyone search through the magazines and clip out what is a goal, a vision, a target or dream. It might be a cruise, Disneyland, a beautiful sunset on a beach, a new car, faster computer, golf clubs, powerful titles or family values. What will their life look like when they *Go Diamond?*
- Have everyone share magazines.
- Have them paste the pictures that they cut out onto the poster board.
- Bring your treasure map to the next event and share it with others.
- Put the treasure map up where you can view it daily, on your daily path.

I-Cans:
In the magazines, cut out pictures of all kinds of eyes, from humans and animals and glue the eyes on the container. Take the can home and put it on your desk, as a pen and pencil holder to remind you that I-CAN *Go Diamond!*

The 80/20 Rule

There is a rule in life that says 20% of the distributors do 80% of the business and 80% do 20%. There is no point to try to change this; it is just the way it is. You can't get rid of the 80% of the distributors who aren't working the business and you don't want to. Why? Because whoever is left, the 20% of them will do 80% of the business and the 80% will do 20%.

This law is something you must understand in Network Marketing. 20% are going to do 80% of the business. It works the same way, year after year. You can't change it.

How can you work this to your advantage?
You can only give 20% of your time to the 80%. Why? Because the 80% are only producing 20% of the results. Give 80% of your time to the top 20% producers who are delivering the 80% of the bottom line.

Guess what will happen?
You will get pulled in the opposite direction. Guess who wants 80% of your time? The wrong group! They are the wrong group in terms of productivity and effectiveness in your business…and for your future.

So now what?
Work individually with the 20% top producers. It's important to only work in groups with the 80%.

Put your focus on your top producers.
Help the top 20% *Go Diamond*! Then the process starts all over again for them. 20% of their successline will produce 80% of the results.

The
Product Launch

When a group of people get together to look at product and to consider joining the opportunity, distributors title it in a variety of ways. It can be called a home party, a show, a demo, a workshop, a grand opening, a presentation, opportunity meeting, a showcase or a Product Launch. In this section, we are going to call it a Product Launch. This is the way Jayne Leach has built her business. The Product Launch has helped propel Jayne to Diamond and we wanted to include it as an idea for you to use as well.

Jan did home parties and once a month trainings, to empower others to use *The Go Diamond System*, so that, they could be independent of her. Jan did not do Product Launches for anyone else, because she did so many home parties a month herself, that she did not have time to do them for others. Jan recruited so many people a month, that she could not have done Launches for her new distributors and done her own maintenance of personal sales as well.

However this method clearly works.

The purpose of a Product Launch is to provide a fast, efficient and duplicatable way of putting a customer base in place. Doing a demonstration for a new distributor is one method of helping them get off to a great start.

Any new business needs to be launched into the market place and in Network Marketing, a Product Launch is a proven and effective method for building a retail customer base and with it, the potential for ongoing repeat sales and referrals. It can generate further Product Launches and prospects who may wish to join the business. The powerful psychological benefit of quickly arranging a Product Launch for a new distributor, is that if they have 10 friends or colleagues turn up for their Launch and most or all of them purchase products, then they are in effect endorsing the new business, and the confidence this gives will be immense. It also has the added benefit of providing an opportunity for their sponsor to coach them on the product range and how to present it. It's quick; fun; time and cost effective, as you are presenting to a number of people at once; and it gets results, so it will pay you to be organized and plan well. It is not necessary to go to all of your distributors' first Product Launches. With *The Go Diamond System*, they should be well trained to do their own. When you have people long distance, you can't be there to do their Product Launch for them, so train them using this system and they should do fantastic.

How to plan the Product Launch using The Five 'P' Formula – Perfect Planning Provides Plenty of Profit.

Arrange a planning session with the new distributor in their first ten days. It's the time spent planning prior to the event, that guarantees a successful and profitable outcome. Here is what to plan with the new distributor:

- **Date and time of event:**
  - Always have your diary (daytimer, filofax) with you, and together agree on two to four event dates for the Product Launches. Friday evenings are less favorable but there is no reason why a Launch cannot be based around *"coffee morning"* times during the week or at weekends. Or any other morning or night of the week. Normally allow 5–7 days between the planning date and the first Launch, in order to give time for prospective guests to be invited. An average Launch takes 45 minutes to one hour. A good start time in the evenings is generally around 8:00 pm and for *"coffee mornings,"* either 10:00 or 11:00 am.

- **Who to invite:**
  - Write down the names of everyone you can think of who may or may not attend. Leave a space between each name for a *"bring-a-friend"*. This will help you remember to encourage guests to bring a friend along to the Launch.
  - Make sure you have between 10-20 or more names on your list. Of course, not everyone invited will be able to attend. Experience shows that only about half of the people invited will turn up. Make sure that people from different groups are invited, to ensure that there are prospective customers, distributors and contacts in different areas.
  - Here is who to include: look at the Memory Jogger on page 41 to see who you can think of to invite.
  - The goal on the day of the Launch is to have a minimum of 8–10 people in attendance, to ensure that the averages for customers purchasing and finding prospective new distributors works in your favor.

· How to invite:

Having written the list, next train the new distributor on how they can invite people to the first Launch:

· The telephone approach:

This is the quickest and most effective way of inviting people to the Launch. When picking up the phone, be enthusiastic and sound excited. This call should be made at least 5 days before the event and might go something like:

"Hi Jan, it's Jayne here. How are you, the family, etc. (a little bit of chit chat). Jan, the reason for the call is that I'm very excited because I've recently started my own business and I'm working with a wonderful range of products. On Tuesday evening at 8:00pm, I'm having a few special friends round to show them what I'm doing and I'd love for you and Bill to be there. Can you make it?"

Or

"Hi Jan, it's Jayne here. How are you, the family, etc. (a little bit of chit chat). I'm having a coffee morning at my home on Thursday at 11:00am, where I'm going to be sharing some information on a wonderful range of...(mention the type of products being marketed, whether it is toys, books, cosmetics, healthcare, nutrition, jewelry, etc.). Come along, we'll have some fun and bring a friend. I'd love you to be there; can you come?"

Or

"Hi Andy, it's John here. How are you, the family, etc. (a little bit of chit chat). Andy, the reason for the call is because Jayne and I are having a few friends to our house on Sunday evening at 8:00 for a glass of wine and 'nibbles', and to launch our new business and the products we're working with. We'd love you and Sue to be there. Can you come?"

If they say, *"I'm sorry, I can't attend because...,"* simply book them into the following Launch and if they can't make that, say something like, *"That's a shame, never mind but I would love to come and show you our products anyway. I've got my diary (day timer, calendar, filofax) here, so can we set a date to get together?"*

Once the calls have been made, mark in the calendar, (filofax) those who have agreed to come and give them a courtesy call, two days before the event. This acts as a memory jog, to remind them to be there and to give you some idea of final numbers.

Examples:

> *"Hi Andy, it's John here. Just a quick call to say how much Jayne and I are looking forward to seeing you and Sue at our place on Sunday evening."*

Or:

> *"Hi Jan, it's Jayne here. Just a quick call to say how much I'm looking forward to seeing you on Thursday. Are you bringing a friend?"*

•The face-to-face approach:

This is for people who regularly come into contact with people who they might want to invite, whether it be at the place of work, the school gates, the gym, at your church or wherever. To be prepared for this approach, have some invitations that have been pre-written with the time and date. Give these out at least five days before the event and remind the guest a couple of days before the event that you are expecting them to attend. Most companies that use a Product Launch, will have pre-printed invitations with the logo on them. If they don't, then buy some bright invitations from the store or design them yourself using your computer.

•Absent Guests:

Always have a few spare product brochures and customer order forms on hand, to give to the people invited but unable to attend the Product Launch. You may be surprised at how many outside orders can be collected. Set a goal to collect three or four orders before the Launch event takes place.

•Product and Literature for the event:

Prepare yourself ahead of the event. On the day of your Launch, have everything you need. Here is what you will need:

•A complete product demonstration kit:

It is so much easier to present the products and their benefits, if you have them to show. Experience tells us that when a customer can touch, smell feel or see a product, there becomes an emotional link to it and they feel they must have it. It's very hard to describe something that is in a brochure, particularly how it feels or smells. Make sure that your kit is clean, is in order, is not old, as this does not give a good impression.

•Literature and information packs.

On the day of your Product Launch demonstration, have order forms and pens, product information brochures, testimonials and fact sheets, business opportunity information packs, company recruiting audio and video, your business cards, a calculator and most importantly your diary, so you are prepared to book further launches or meetings with potential new distributors.

•**The day of your launch:**

  •Even though you may be feeling a little nervous prior to the event, you have to remember that it is your excitement and energy at the demonstration, which will make or break the event. Nobody wants to *"buy"* from somebody who is miserable and worried, so smile and be enthusiastic and excited. And have fun.

  •First impressions count. Be well groomed and be sure that your demonstration products are clean and ready for use. Arrive 15-30 minutes before the event, to help set up the display with your new Distributor; to discuss who is coming and who from their guest list is most likely to be interested in the business opportunity. The demonstration kit should be displayed nicely, maybe on a coffee table or a flat surface of some kind and you may well want to use a nice cloth to cover the table, before you build your display. Keep it simple so it looks easy to do and duplicatable. If you have samples of the products, have them on the display.

  •Have information packs laid out and ready to give to the guests. This could include a recruiting brochure, a brochure of what is in the kit, the kit request form, order forms, catalogs or anything that will give people an idea of what your company opportunity is and how they can easily join.

  •Keep refreshments simple and inexpensive; tea, coffee, soft drinks and biscuits (cookies) are ample or if it's a more social event, maybe wine and soft drinks. Refrain from lavish food and drink, as prospective distributors and future Product Launch hosts, may feel daunted by the prospect of having to do the same. Serve refreshments on guest arrival or at the end but never during the Launch, as it is very distracting and disrupts the flow.

  •Arrange not to have distractions such as pets, children or cell phones and turn off the TV and your cell phone.

  •As the guests arrive, if you are there as the upline, have your new distributor introduce you and enthusiastically help greet all of the guests. Have the new distributor hand each guest an information package.

  •Start the presentation within 15 minutes of the time arranged and do not wait for latecomers. Do not penalize those who are there early to wait on those who come late.

•**The presentation and what to say:**

  •First relax, smile and look as if you are enjoying yourself. People are not there to be lectured; all you are doing is sharing some information with them. The new distributor makes an opening statement by thanking the host/hostess and the guests for attending, then briefly explain why they joined the company, and then introduce their sponsor, to run the Launch.

•The new distributor now listens to what the sponsor says. This is part of their training. The distributor only gets involved with the presentation when asked, and when doing so, must be very positive and enthusiastic.

•**As the training sponsor, you will:**

•Briefly share about your background and why you are doing the business, highlighting some key benefit points that are relevant to the potential distributor prospects in the room.

•Briefly explain a little about the company's history and track record, their standing in the market place and any other key benefits that are relevant to prospective distributors.

•Briefly explain the benefits of the products, backed up by stories. Specification tells, stories and benefits sell.

•Invite prospects to get involved by trying the products and seeing for themselves how they work. Keep it fun, encouraging everyone to get involved. Everyone needs to feel that they have had a good time, are happy to use and own your products.

•When you have finished the presentation, thank everyone for attending and supporting the new distributor, then invite them to order the products which most appealed to them, by completing the order form, explaining the methods of payment. Ask if there is anyone in the room who would support the new distributor by having a Launch in their home and tell them that they will get some free product if they do so.

•Encourage the guests to *"play"* with the products while you and the new distributor leave the room for a few minutes to go and get refreshments. This gives the guests a space and time to think which products they would like to order.

•When you come back into the room, circulate and ask each of the guests which product they would like to invest in and answer any of their questions. Focus on the guests that the new distributor has pointed out as being potential prospects. Start a conversation with them, asking fact-finding questions that will lead to suggesting that they get involved in the business. Give them a business pack and ask for their phone number. Be ready for a follow-up call to make an appointment to meet. After having taken all the orders and explained the delivery details, thank the guests again for coming and supporting the Launch of the new distributor's business. Depart and leave the distributor to finish the event with their friends.

•The day after the presentation:

> •Contact the new distributor who held the Launch, the very next day. This is a call, to review the previous night and talk through the event.
>
> •How much was finally purchased and what that means in terms of profit, is almost always exciting, as very often the new distributor will be totally surprised at how much the total is.
>
> •Follow up on guests that you think could be outstanding in the business. Have the new distributor call and give a compliment of saying that the sponsor thought they would be great doing what you do. Ask for availability to meet to discuss the business further. If prospects had fun at the Launch and enjoyed the products, they will agree to meet and now you have a potential new distributor. This can often result in two or three new team members per Launch.
>
> •Schedule further planning meetings, trainings or events, recap on the ordering procedure and payment details to the company. Chat about any other business and agree on what happens next.
>
> •Plan their next Launch.

The new distributor will quickly feel comfortable to run their own Launch and also that of their new team members. This coaching time is vital to you and the growth of the distributor. The faster they learn how to do it by themselves, the sooner you can go and start someone else. How many times will the new distributor need to see and be coached until they can do it on their own? We all learn at different rates but hopefully once. With *The Go Diamond System*, they will be able to do their own Launches very quickly. Competence usually happens earlier than the new distributor feels, so you as their sponsor need to *"let go"* sooner rather than later, and give the new distributor wings, so as not to develop a dependency challenge.

The average Launch will be capable of producing hundreds of pounds or dollars worth of product movement to end users. It is clear to see that it is a great generator of income with people wanting to make between £150 to £1200 (around $200 to $1,500) a month.

Depending on your company's products, the Product Launch is something that men and women can both do. This is one way to do Network Marketing. The goal is for every distributor to have a group of happy, satisfied customers purchasing at retail, and new distributors constantly joining.

Share a wealth of Information

The *Go Diamond* Glossary of Terms

Abundance= What you will attract to your life when you help enough other people get what they want.

Accelerate= Making the process of getting to *Going Diamond,* go faster.

Activity= Doing the *Go Diamond* fundamentals over and over.

Approach= in day to day life, just sharing the opportunity with anyone you know, even strangers.

Average= As close to the bottom as to the top.

But= **B**ehold **U**nderlying **T**houghts. Whatever comes after this word is the truth.

Build= To build upon a system that brings a residual income, forever.

Care= To be empathetic to distributors and sincerely want them to succeed.

Character= Who you are when you are alone. Being in integrity and going for greatness, while never hurting another fellow human being along the way.

Compensation Plan=This is the company pay plan. It's how companies compensate distributors for moving product from the warehouse to the public. Percentages are paid out at different levels of the plan. You are compensated for your effort of bringing people in to the business and for your own personal sales. The major goal is to get to the top position of the company compensation plan.

Confidence=Having the self-confidence that takes you from being average to *Going Diamond.*

Decision= Just deciding.

Determination= Being unstoppable.

Direction= Always heading for Diamond.

Discipline= Doing the fundamentals over and over again. Not letting distractions get in your way of *Going Diamond.*

Dream stealers= Those who do not want you to succeed.

Empowerment= To encourage others to believe in themselves.

Excuse= Your productivity will either promote you or expose you.

Failure= To quit or give up on your goals, visions and dreams. Not an option.

Fire Up!= It's the passion in your heart, head and mind, that keeps you going. It's an attitude.

Fun= Have fun on your journey.

Goals=Your decisions deep down, what you are willing to work for.

Gratitude Attitude= Being thankful everyday for your blessings.

Growth= Can be measured by money, products moved, and/or personal growth.

Happily involve=This is when someone decides to join you as a distributor, have a presentation for you or to become a customer. Getting people happily involved with the product and opportunity is the key to success. We don't want people who we have to beg to do the business; we want distributors who want to do the business.

Help= Guiding others to go up the compensation plan; help enough other people succeed and you will get everything you dream of.

Hunger= Wanting something so badly that you take action to get it.

Increase= The more you increase your knowledge, the better leader you will be. The more you increase your successline by bringing in more distributors and helping them become leaders, the more money you will earn.

Ignite= Get on fire with desire; share your passion with others.

Impossible= Act as if it is impossible to fail. It's an attitude.

Improve= Keep being a student of those who are living the lifestyle you want.

Influence= Inspiring others to a better life.

Information Package=This is a package of information such as a catalog, recruiting brochure, tape, video or any information that you can put together to hand a prospect or to send them in the mail (post).

Knowledge= When you learn information which you did not know that you did not know.

Leadership= Leading distributors to information and to success strategies. Helping others achieve their dreams.

Lie= Not telling ourselves the truth.

Motivate= You can only motivate yourself; no one can motivate you. Motivation comes from within.

Multi Level Marketing= A payment system that is on several levels and includes personal growth and development.

Network Marketing= A payment system that is based on people sharing products and an opportunity.

No= Take out of your vocabulary.

No Limits= Taking yourself as far as you wish. It's an attitude.

Opinion= Just someone's thoughts. Evaluate them and form your own opinions.

Passion= Giving it all you have because you want to. Ignite it and keep it going forever.

Past= Something that happened one second ago that is not attached to what you will do in the future.

Prospect= A suspect who may be interested in your opportunity.

Prosperity= What you will get when you *Go Diamond.* A life filled with prosperity.

Poverty= Not necessary.

Quality= What you give in life to others. What you are willing to work for to get in life.

Reading= Readers are leaders and leaders are readers.

Referrals= When someone gives you a name of a person who might be interested in getting happily involved. Follow up is the key. When some one says *"no"* to your opportunity, always ask who THEY might know who would like to get involved and follow up.

Rock= What stabilizes you during tough times.

Time= What we are willing to work for= time freedom.

Training= When you train enough people who can train others in *The Go Diamond System,* your business will have explosive growth.

Truth= What we think is real for us. Might be totally different for others. Perception is everything.

Until= You will march towards Diamond ***until*** you get there.

Value= What you love in life. Key to wealth; *help enough other people get what they value* and you will have more abundance than you ever dreamed of.

Wealth= What you will get if you help enough other people get what they want.

Wish= A dream without a deadline.

Yes= The Diamond attitude.

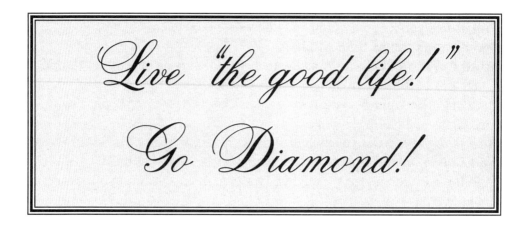

Section 3 ....

Train the System

Decide to Become a Master Trainer

When people join Network Marketing, they are choosing a product and an opportunity to sell. The business does not take off unless product is moved. The idea is to have thousands of distributors moving product. You can start the process by just sponsoring one person and asking them to do the same. Get several people who have been sponsored by you, choosing to do the same process.

Network Marketing kicks in when you can get a system to share what is possible with your distributors. The people who really want to *Go Diamond* are those who are obsessed with getting to the top. They only listen to people who can share with them methods, systems and ideas, that work. They don't listen to distributors who are not taking massive action.

Get a simple system that everyone can use, that can be used over and over and over again and that immediately captures distributor's attention. It gives them confidence that they can train their own new distributors and not be dependent on the upline to do the trainings for them.

There are distributors who believe that they are the best trainers in the successline and they value being identified as super trainers. That's what they are, super trainers. They are not master Network Marketers. **The Master Trainers have learned to build leaders and to make them independent leaders of their own successlines.** The Master Trainers work hard at instilling confidence and enthusiasm into the successline and showing others how to build their own businesses. When you have enough independent leaders all building their own successlines, you will *Go Diamond*. It's not hard to do. It's not easy either. It takes time, patience, commitment, desire and, an understanding of all of the *Go Diamond* Gems shared in this book.

Start your own personal growth and development program. Be a student of Network Marketing. Build your library and read, read and read. Feed your mind. When you build your vocabulary, you are able to communicate more effectively and distributors will gravitate towards you to listen to you. When you take massive action and get massive results, distributors will listen to you. When you start the process of building a Network Marketing business and you don't start and stop, or back off or give in, and instead stay positive, motivated, and inspired until you *Go Diamond*, your credibility will soar. You can't stroll to Diamond. It's got to be a serious decision. To *Go Diamond*, Master how to train others in a simple way, to work the business. A Master Trainer wants their distributors up in front of the room training. You will rarely see a Master Trainer in the front of the room. They are working daily to help distributors understand the big picture and to give them plenty of space to be creative and build their own successlines.

The biggest successlines have yet to be built. There is more room than you can imagine for new and bigger and better success stories in Network Marketing. If you do not have a success story YET, then use the story of how your upline got to Diamond and that you are following their training. When you use *The Go Diamond System* all over your country or the world, you have done your job. You will be a Master in Network Marketing. You will have the top title in your company's compensation plan.

Becoming a Master Trainer takes practice. It takes persistence. It is all about duplicating the strategies and activities of those who are at the top. There are no exact ways to train. Jan has done *The Go Diamond System* for over two decades and Jayne's organization has had explosive growth since using it.

Jan used it in her home in Dallas, Texas, month after month. Then she took it on the road all over the United States and her successline flourished. It's like giant flashcards. Just pass them out to distributors who attend your training and let them teach each other by using the visual flashcards or storyboards. Use the training over and over again. Distributors will gain confidence and will say, *"I can do that training, and I can do it as well or better than those sharing the information today!"* Once they shift to thinking they can do it, they will have more confidence in recruiting or sponsoring others into their successline.

When you build your team, think recruiting. Then, immediately what follows recruiting is teaching/training/coaching/mentoring others to do the same. Once you have this system in place, day by day, event by event, training by training, your successline will begin to grow and prosper. It's simply making a decision to decide to become a Master Trainer.

If we achieved the top position using this information, so can you. We believe in you. Go for it all; go for having the lifestyle, for abundance and prosperity. It's waiting for you on a silver platter. Come to the table of plenty. We have a place already set for you. Focus your energy on training others to do the fundamentals over and over again. We wish you speedy success.

Life is too short for anything less than the very best the world has to offer.

What is Training and Why Does it Work?

Many distributors go to seminars, read books, and listen to hours of tapes. So much of the information they get is fantastic and the tips can change their life and business forever. Even after all the personal growth and development, most distributors do not move their business ahead. This is the sad truth. Here is why. **Information alone won't build a successline.**

There are many distributors in Network Marketing who *"know"* how to build a thriving successline. They KNOW how, yet, they don't do it. They stick around for years, knowing what to do but don't take action to build a successline. Want to know how to get your distributors to take action, be accountable, not get tired, not drop out, and instead take massive, consistent action? Want them to develop into leaders? You can do it. Old training methods just don't work fast enough; until now! Until you found *The Go Diamond System.*

Training doesn't start and stop. It's an on-going process that helps distributors take action and work on their skills every day. The Upline (the person who sponsors a person) starts a relationship as the trainer from the first conversation with the new distributor. It starts with the very first communication the two have together. The new distributor trusts the person who sponsors them (the Upline) and wants to succeed. With that trust, the new distributor will listen and pay attention to the sponsor. Here is what normally happens. The sponsor doesn't know how to have a synergistic relationship with the new distributor and the new distributor figures this out. Distrust then sets in. Now the relationship between the Upline as trainer and the new distributor results in non-communication and disappointment. Make a partnership with the person you sponsor. The sponsor has a vested interest in making sure that the new distributor succeeds. The sponsor is responsible to each person they sponsor, to see that they get started on the right track. This does not mean that the sponsor is responsible for each new distributor's success; only the new distributor can take that responsibility.

The new distributor is accountable to the Upline so that they stay on the path to achieving their goals and dreams. Training is like a *"seminar in action."* It helps your distributors learn and then apply what they have learned to create activity each day. The more productive the new distributor is in the beginning, the more enthusiastic the distributor will be during their career. Each time the distributor learns one of the *Go Diamond* Gems, confidence increases. With confidence comes results. With confidence, distributors go into motion. When motion happens, promotion happens. Results begin to stack upon results. The distributor finds their own style and with their confidence, they begin to take risks and with risks comes more understanding. With more understanding, more information, more communication, more leadership and more training, the distributor can make the decision for themselves to become the Upline, leader, coach, or trainer. You have become a Master Trainer when you have leveraged your time by training others to have the confidence, wisdom and information to train others. The great news is, you can do daily trainings, or mini-seminars online, by doing a Daily Inspiration (an email message containing one *Go Diamond* Gem a day) or by having your own webpage with on-going training on it, or voice mail blasts with regular information or with teleconferencing calls that help distributors continue to gather information.

Your success depends upon your being able to develop distributors and duplicate your own efforts. It's not important to be the company trainer, to be the speaker for your company, to be flown around the world or your country to *"speak."* Do not attach significance to this. That is not true Network Marketing. True Master Trainers concentrate on building their OWN businesses. They don't have time to focus on building the entire company. Many companies want their top distributors to speak for free, and to train the rest of the company. Once a distributor seeks this kind of recognition and attaches significance to this, they are now into what satisfies their ego and they take their focus off building their own successline and are no longer Master Trainers…..they are only underpaid speakers. However, for the Master Trainer, the benefits are fantastic when you decide to be a Master at *training your own distributors in your successline.* Here are a few to note:

- You get faster growth; your successline will grow fast.
- You get partnerships/relationships with distributors who will duplicate your style.

- You get a trusting relationship with your distributors that will make them accountable to you.
- You get to inspire others and watch them grow and prosper.
- You get to share your experiences and wisdom that will help your distributors have confidence and courage to take massive action.
- You get to share what you have learned in your own personal growth and development program.
- You get to duplicate yourself and leverage your time, by training others how to train their own distributors.
- You get more free time in your life and less stress, because not only are you training distributors but, also, you have distributors training the duplicatable system to their distributors.
- You get reduced stress because you have Mastered Training others and have more balance in your life.
- You get high quality people to join your successline.
- You get more time to focus on achieving your own goals.
- You get to use your own creativity.
- You get an amazing fulfillment of watching others achieve their visions and dreams.

Can anyone be a Master Trainer?

You can if you have the ability to listen to others and have a sincere desire to help distributors personally grow and achieve greatness in THEIR lives. If you just want to stand up and talk on a stage or in a room, and you cannot and do not come from contribution, you will not be known as a Master Trainer. You must come from how you can contribute to the lives of your distributors. It's not what you know, it's what you show. You don't have to be a *"know it all"* to be a Master Trainer. The *Diamond* to-be figures out that they really are trainers early on in their career. They have followed systems of ideas and skills that bring out the best in their distributors. They have done the same systems over and over again and have gotten amazing results. Set up your own *"Training System"* to use in your own successline.

How to Train your Successline:

Do this: #1: Make a decision to be the Master Trainer of your own successline. Here is how: have a conversation with yourself. Are you committed, ready and willing to become a Master Trainer? Distributors are either attracted to the idea of being Master Trainers or they are not. If you are, the next step is to begin to sponsor new distributors into your successline who would like to be trained. Start with five new distributors. Start with a small number. This will give you the opportunity to master *The Go Diamond System*. Then as you do several duplicatable trainings, you will see that those first five distributors will see how easy it is to sponsor others and to then train them. Then you will want to add more distributors to the process and continue training them. Do this process over and over again. You will be astonished at your results.

Next, do this: #2: With your successline growing, identify the distributors in your successline who are serious about building their own successline. Initiate a conversation with them about becoming Master Trainers of their own successlines. The idea is that you want several front level leaders doing their own *Go Diamond* trainings.

Next, do this: #3: Express your expectations of what you expect from your training. Ask your leaders what they expect of you. Get clear on your mutual expectations so that you can create a successful partnership relationship. You are the Upline. To be a fantastic Upline, you must have trained distributors who seek to become leaders.

Next do this: #4: Set up weekly communications with your leaders, thirty minutes maximum in time and agree to work together for the next three months. Then you will want to see their results. For those who follow your training, they will get results. Then you let them be their own trainers and start looking for the next leaders to put into your next three month training program. During these thirty minute calls, go through this book, chapter by chapter. Give the leaders on the call homework to do, to read a book and to do a book report on it and fax that report to you. Readers are leaders and leaders are readers.

And finally do this: #5: Set up individual calls with those leaders who are on fire with desire and who are taking action. Help them work through challenges and roadblocks and give them support by sharing the knowledge that you are learning through your own personal development. Want a thriving business? Then focus on building leaders and making THEM successful. The more successful your leaders are, the faster you will *Go Diamond*.

What do I do in a Training Session?

In every training session, have products set up. Have *The Go Diamond System* storyboards ready and hand them out to each distributor at the training. Ask each distributor which card they would like to train from or hand them out randomly. Get the new distributor to get involved right away in the training mode. Once they use the story boards to get started, they can *"see"* themselves as trainers and off they will go to build their own successlines. The more cards they can use at trainings, the more their confidence will grow. Talk about the benefits of the products, have testimonials, have photos or photo albums that show photos of the incentive trips. Have distributors share what is selling and how they sold products last week or last month. Be enthusiastic at your trainings. Have someone tell their own success story. Let them shine. Start and end on time. End with a call to action. Here is how:

Ask those at the training to come up with ten goals that they want to achieve in the next ninety days. Suggest fun goals as well as business goals. Ask these questions:

"Are your goals what you really want or do you feel like you 'should' or 'have to' achieve these goals?"
"Are they your real goals or what you think I want to hear?"
"If there were no barriers, where would you want to be in ninety days?"

Diamonds know no barriers. They will not be denied. Help distributors re-evaluate their goals, so they feel their goals are what they really want to achieve; what they must achieve. Have them turn their shoulds and coulds into *"musts."*

Make sure that there are fun goals on the list. Why? Because by including goals that are fun and easy to achieve, the distributor will feel inspired and energized to tackle the more challenging ones.

Here is a form that you might want to use during your trainings. Give this to your distributors during the meeting to fill in and return to you.

The positive thinker learns how to knock the "t" off of "can't."

What I really want to do in the next 30 days:

_____

_____

What I have accomplished since the last training:

_____

_____

The challenges I am working on right now:

_____

_____

The opportunities in front of me now:

_____

_____

What I am here for today:

_____

_____

What I promise to do before the next training:

_____

_____

Being a Master Trainer is:

Taking Massive Action and Developing Leaders:

Training works on two levels. The first level is to have distributors take consistent action and stay accountable to their own goals. The second level is supporting the distributors in their own personal development, to start developing skills, ideas and confidence, so that they can become the trainers of their own successline. Training can help distributors use their own creative ability. Distributors will begin to trust you as the Trainer because you listen to them, you do not talk down to them or talk at them. You care, you want them to succeed beyond their own expectations. Help distributors get clear on the fact that they must go to work on changing themselves to adapt to building a large, successful and thriving business. By developing leaders, you are helping distributors to accomplish their own goals.

As you develop leaders, you are developing yourself. As the leader goes, so does the successline.

Simplifying your Training by getting focused on being duplicatable:

In today's world, it seems that trying to build a business while working around a job or family life is very demanding and overwhelming, too demanding, too hard or just not worth it. Here are ideas to help you do it all:

- Ask distributors to do research on fairs and booths and trade shows and to present the opportunities to the distributors at the next meeting and collect money from everyone to cover the investment of the event.
- Be careful about what you commit your time to. When you do commit, commit 100%.
- Be willing to say the word "*No*" more. Only commit yourself to just a few things in life.
- Cut your "to do" list down to no more than eight activities per day.
- Delegate more responsibilities to your leaders. This empowers them and you will be surprised at the talent in your successline. Have distributors organize the next successline event. Ask 3-5 top leaders to each be accountable for presenting *The Go Diamond System* and filling the meeting room or home to do a training; you will pop by to say hello to all of their new distributors.
- Do it, dump it or delegate it.
- Empower your leaders by letting them run the meetings and trainings. Stand at the back of the room and cheer them on. The sooner you are not running the meetings and trainings, the sooner you will become a Diamond. Let your leaders run the meetings. You do not want to always be running from meeting to meeting or training to training. That is NOT being a Master Trainer. You want to start living the lifestyle of the *Diamond* position as soon as possible. If you have messed up the last several years of your life and have not done this, it's time to make some massive changes and get clear on what being a Master Trainer really is.....someone who can build a Network Marketing business, and leave it for two months and it doesn't skip a beat. Why? Because you have leaders in place who are running their own successlines completely on their own, without needing you. That's when you get to enjoy the abundant lifestyle of the *Diamond*.
- You can do it all. You can build a business even if you only have pockets of time to give it. It does not have to be a 24/7/365 type of business.
- Only focus on your family and business and say *"No"* to anything else that takes time away from your focus.
- It is better to be productive in just a couple of areas of life, than to be unproductive in many.
- Hire a housekeeper and someone to do the laundry. Delegate whatever you dislike doing.
- Hire an assistant or an older child to watch your children for a couple

of hours a day or week, where you can watch what is going on while you focus on building your business.

•Lighten your load. Have very little in your office out on display.

•Look for ways to organize your life. Get a filing system.

•Allocate an area for your books and tapes and from your first book, call this your LIBRARY.

•Get a computer, get online, and get software programs that can help you manage your business.

•MBP= **M**anage **B**y **P**iles. Put things into stacks and give the stacks priority. This stack is Priority #1, #2, #3, etc. Then go to work on Stack #1 and get through it. Have a huge trash can and pitch what you can right into that can. Have a stack of manila folders and file away what you want to keep. Try to touch every piece of paper only once.

•Take care of yourself and you will have more to give to others. Really take care of yourself. The more you do, the more you can accomplish.

Don't put up with settling:

Don't settle or tolerate mediocrity. When you lose focus, change your focus or get distracted, the building of the business will slow down and you will not *Go Diamond*. If something needs fixing, get it fixed. If you do not have a workspace where you are uninterrupted, get one. If your phone is always ringing, clearly you need a voice mail system to capture those calls. You don't want that phone to be at your ear all day. That's not freedom. What about all those leads on your desk that you need to contact? What about distributors you have trained and hope will go into leadership but who don't follow through with their promises? What about the distributors who complain or gossip? What about the distributors who feel the need to check in with you but aren't taking action? What about the distributors who want you to be their new best friend? What about tolerating family and friends or spouses who are negative and try to take your focus off building your business?

Why tolerate any of this? Do you know what the cost is of tolerating too much in your life? (So you won't hurt someone else? So you will not be seen as a workaholic? So you will think you are more balanced? So you won't rock the boat? So you are not viewed as selfish? So you will feel needed?)

The cost is great. When we settle, and when we tolerate, we are drained, tired and frustrated and can become negative. We are robbed of energy and ultimately our business becomes less important and we lose our passion and our motivation and drive for *Going Diamond*.

You may fear that, if you don't tolerate or put up with settling for where you are in your life, you might lose your friends or relationships. But ask yourself: are these people in my life my true friends? Are my relationships healthy if I tolerate people in my life who are holding me back? How is settling and tolerating affecting my feelings, passion, time, enthusiasm, commitments for going for greatness, true goals, visions, dreams, peace of mind and my financial independence? Settling does not serve me. It's not that I am selfish; it's that I no longer want barriers. I seek a life of abundance and prosperity and will settle for nothing less.

Be driven and achieve your goals and you will not be denied. **Nothing is wrong with that.** Fabulous lifestyles await those who will not be pulled down, pulled out, give up or be denied. It's the fire of desire that nothing and no one can put out. It's the passion that will keep you going, not settling, not tolerating any more. You have had enough of that life; you are ready to step into your own magnificence. To build a healthy future, healthy successline, and to have empowering relationships with others, take a good hard look at what you are putting up with.

Imagine how great your life and business would be if you chose to no longer settle or tolerate what you are putting up with right now. Work on not tolerating interruptions anymore. It might take some time, but start today not settling for a mediocre life. Don't worry about taking action on all of them at the same time; just start with a few and go to work on making some major changes.

When you decide to be a Master Trainer, place yourself on the fast track to *Going Diamond.* Spend the majority of your time developing five major, powerful leaders who are coaching and developing the rest of your successline. Seek to implement *The Go Diamond System* into your own successline. It is a thrilling and rewarding experience that will bring you a lifestyle of prosperity and abundance. Being a Master Trainer is powerful. It works like magic, like a miracle, if you are willing to just work on your skills. It starts today!

> Within you right now is the power to do things you never dreamed possible. This power becomes available to you just as soon as you can change your limiting beliefs.

 Diamond Tip: Don't be average; be a champion.

The *Go Diamond* System

The need for a duplicatable training system was so apparent to Jan when she first started in Network Marketing, that she quickly developed her own simple system. She relentlessly applied and coached her team to do the same. This resulted in her becoming the top distributor in her company, a position she still holds today, in addition to being a world-class trainer and author. Jayne was already at the top of her company's compensation plan when she was introduced to Jan's original system. Jayne began using it and shared it with her top leaders around the world, with startling great results: bonus checks doubling, tripling and quadrupling within months; positions being achieved faster than ever and confident leaders developing more quickly.

This system is fun to use, and is so simple that anyone can do it. It is proven to work in several countries and can be used as both a sponsoring system and training system.

All new distributors need basic information so that they can get started as quickly as possible.

This training system is flexible, fun, and adaptable to the group or person being trained. It can be used successfully on a one-to-one basis, in small and large groups, everywhere! It is duplicatable and consists of the fundamental basics for those who want to succeed and progress quickly up their company's compensation plan.

Use this system daily, weekly, fortnightly or monthly (as appropriate) at your 1–2 hour training.

Have fun and enjoy the training. The more you use and duplicate this system, the faster you will *Go Diamond!* Nothing compares with the view from the top!

Location of Training

•Always have trainings in the SAME location and on the SAME day and time, so that it becomes a business discipline or habit for distributors to expect to have new guests and their new distributors at each event.
•Remember to promote the time and location on a regular basis.
•The most effective venues are in the home but the system can be used in a coffee shop, hotel or meeting room; anywhere that people can gather together on a regular basis.
•When several key leaders work together with larger group numbers, a more neutral location may be found to be necessary. This joining together can have the advantage of creating more energy, fun, information, and being less time consuming for each individual leader.

Training Welcome

•Have all distributors and guests fill out your registration/attendance book, stating their name, phone number, email address and the name of the person who invited them.
•Communicate with people at your training by using their first name. Have name tags for everyone and get them to write their first name only with a black marker pen.
•When greeting new people, introduce them to the training leader, sharing details of their background and successes in the business.
•Introduce guests and new distributors to others in the room, making them feel welcome.
•Serve refreshments before and after but never during the training.
•Train your own distributors until new competent leaders emerge. This will ensure fast duplication, with a strong and consistent message.
•Invite your guests to arrive 15 minutes earlier than you plan to start, and always start on time.
•Introduce yourself by saying your name, and by briefly telling why you joined the business. Share with them that you will be available to answer questions at the end of the training. Introduce other leaders in the room who will be helping you with the training.
•Have everyone else briefly introduce themselves.
•Thank everyone for attending and begin the training.

The "Story Board" Training

•Put this training onto giant "Story Boards" (cards approximately 28" x 22" / 71cm x 55cm). Use blue and black markers. Make sure that you do them by hand and not done professionally, as you want your successline to be able to duplicate you. Never do anything other people can't copy.

•Number your giant "Story Board" cards; decide which speaker will present each section and then go through the cards in order–it's so simple. Just follow the words on the cards, having fun as you do so.

•The cards provide the outline for your training, keeping you on course.

•The simplicity of this training will enable you to quickly get your new distributors presenting the "Story Board" cards alongside you. The best-trained distributors are trained on the opportunity and the product. The quicker they participate and have fun, the faster they will become your leaders, the quicker your business will duplicate and grow.

> *Reach the pinnacle*
>
> *of success...*
>
> *Go Diamond!*

 Diamond Tip: Teach your leaders to do this training. It's a proven way to *Go Diamond*.

Story Board #1

For the Trainer: Explain the importance of needing people like the people at the training. Here is what to put on the board:

We need people like you!

We need:
•Energetic and enthusiastic people to help our team grow. People like you!

•You are important to our company growth and to me!

•We need you to succeed!

Story Board #2

For the Trainer: Explain why your company chooses to distribute products using Network Marketing instead of traditional sales and distribution channels. Here is what to put on the board:

CUTTING OUT THE MIDDLEMAN

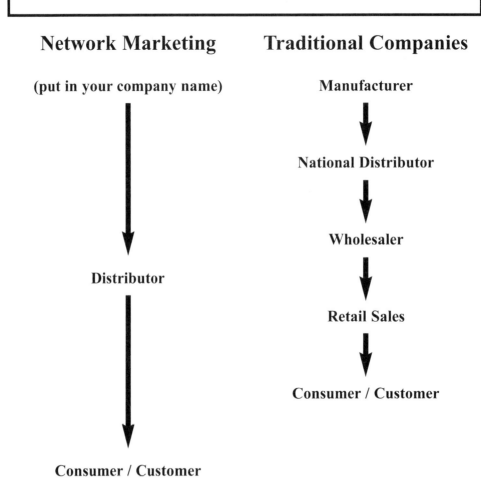

Network Marketing

(put in your company name)

Distributor

Consumer / Customer

Traditional Companies

Manufacturer

National Distributor

Wholesaler

Retail Sales

Consumer / Customer

- Greater customer service
- More efficient business
- More rewarding business
- More motivational to distributors

Story Board #3

For the trainer: Sell the benefits of Network Marketing.
Here is what to put on the board:

The Benefits of the Network Marketing Industry:

✓ **Fast growing industry**

✓ **You are an independent contractor**

✓ **You are your own boss**

✓ **Residual income**

✓ **Great training**

✓ **Tax advantages**

✓ **Team support**

✓ **Flexible hours**

✓ **Unlimited income potential**

✓ **Minimum investment**

✓ **Amazing incentive benefits (travel, car programs, recognition and prizes)**

Story Board #4

For the Trainer: Explain the benefits of being involved in your company. Keep it simple. What are the benefits to the people listening? Focus on them, and don't think about or talk about yourself. Talk about the benefits to **those who are listening**. Sell the benefits. Sell the benefits. Sell the benefits. Here is what to put on the board:

Who is_____(insert your company name here)_____**?**

- **Founded in** (put in your company's start year)

- **Well Managed**

- **Annual Sales**

- **Track Record**

- **Expected Growth**

- **Any other information relevant to your company**

Story Board #5

For the Trainer: Explain the big picture.
Here is what to put on the board:

Traditional Company Pyramid = lots of room at the bottom, but little room at the top!

VS.

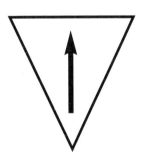

Network Marketing = anyone can move to the top!

Pyramid Example: Least paid employee vs. CEO

Network Marketing Example: New distributor vs. Diamond

180

Story Board #6

For the Trainer: Explain the main reasons why people join the business. Everybody's "why" is different. Facts tell; stories sell.
Here is what to put on the board:

Time Freedom
Extra money
Lifestyle
Pension
Work from home
Debt freedom
Financial freedom
Fun
Meeting new people
Personal development
Achievement
Helping others
Making a difference
Own boss
Incentives (trips/prizes)
Recognition
Peace of Mind

Story Board #7

For the Trainer: Explain the four key fundamentals to building a Network Marketing business. EMPHASIZE the simplicity.
Here is what to put on the board:

Here are the Main FOUR STEPS you are expected to do:

1. Use the products =

Become your own best customer. Buy at wholesale, don't buy products at the store. Replace the products in your home with your own products.

2. Share the products =

Share the benefits of the products and opportunity with others.

3. Build a successline =

Talk to lots of people and share your unique business opportunity. Show them how they can get happily involved right away.

4. Train the successline to do the same =

Train your successline how to use the products, share the products and build their own successline using *The Go Diamond System.*

Story Board #8

For the Trainer: Explain how to get off to a great start!
Here is what to put on the board:

---

1. Make a list of 100 people to contact.

2. Attend a *Go Diamond* Training.

3. Begin to be a user of your products.

4. Attend Team Monthly/Weekly Meetings.

5. Learn about the products and opportunity.

6. Throw out all competing products in your home.

7. Schedule your first presentation as soon as possible.

8. Pinpoint the first 3 people who would want to do what you are doing.

9. Recruit someone in your first 48 hours.

10. Read company material.

11. Join your successline email loop/voicemail.

12. Start a personal growth and development program. (read and listen to tapes or CD's)

Story Board #9

For the Trainer: Explain how to build a successline by harnessing the power of duplication. Here is what to put on the board:

Duplicate Yourself

Grow Your Business

- **You introduce 2 people** = **2**

- **Help those 2 each get 2** = **4**

- **Help those 4 each get 2** = **8**

- **Help those 8 each get 2** = **16**

- **Total** **30**

- **But you personally only found and sponsored the first 2!**

Story Board #10

For the Trainer: Explain exponential growth: 5 x 5 x 5 x 5.
Get totally on fire with desire! Here is what to put on the board:

Teach 5 to Reach 5

You recruit just 5 new distributors   =   5

You teach 5 to reach 5   =   25

Equals   = 125

The next step is to teach 125 to reach 5   = 625

Not including you, that's 780 new distributors in your successline. You get a bonus on the total team sales from your successline.

Take it a step further:

Teach 625 to reach 5 and you get over 3,000 people in your successline!

It's simply mathematical!!!!!!!!!

Story Board #11

For the Trainer: Explain the over all idea of what a compensation plan is. Here is what to put on the board:

What is the ___(insert the name of your company here)___
Compensation Plan?

- **The formula by which we are all paid.**

- **The ladder to success.**

- **All start at the beginning and quickly progress to the top position in the plan.**

- **Achieve each level through personal and total team volume.**

- **Team volume measured in _____.**
  (whatever your company uses as the measure)

Story Board #12

For the Trainer: Explain the start of the compensation plan. Draw circles for the new/prospective distributor to see the power of duplication. Here is what to put on the board:

(entry level title and any qualification required)

YOU

• You get ___% on your personal sales

• You get ___% on_____.

(Put in the title for the first level receiving leadership bonus and qualification requirement)

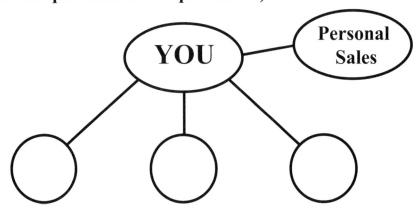

• You get ___% your personal sales

• You get___% on distributors under you.

• You get ___% any other way your company gives percentages.

Story Board #13

For the Trainer: Talk about the benefits of helping your distributors develop their own successline. Here is what to put on the board:

(Put in the title for the next level receiving leadership bonus and qualification requirement)

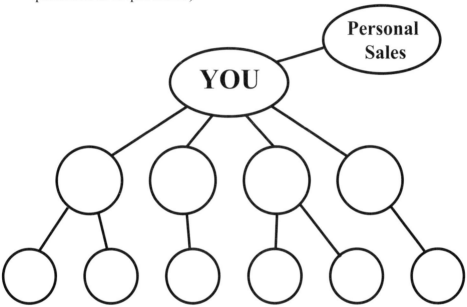

- **You get __% on your personal sales**
- **You get __% on distributors or levels under you.**
- **You get __% any other company ways of earning a bonus.**

Typical monthly income _____

Network Marketing Duplication Begins!

Story Board #14

For the Trainer: Explain how to get to the top pay position in the compensation plan. Here is what to put on the board:

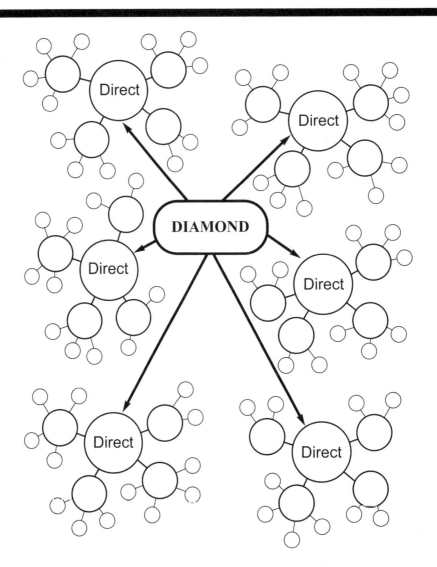

- **You get___% as a bonus at the end of the month on your personal sales**

- **You get ___% on all distributors or levels under you.**

Typical monthly income_____

Story Board #15

For the Trainer: Explain residual income. Income that continues to grow the rest of your life. Explain Royalty Bonus or whatever terminology your company uses for your bonus check. Here is what to put on the board:

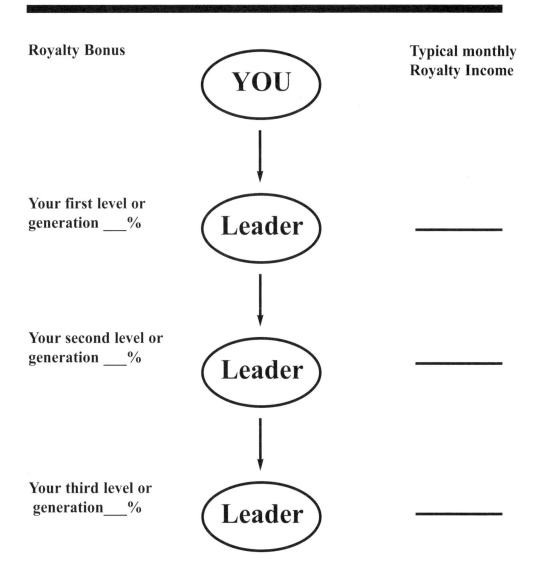

Royalty Bonus

Typical monthly Royalty Income

YOU

Your first level or generation ___%

Leader

Your second level or generation ___%

Leader

Your third level or generation___%

Leader

Imagine if you had 5 lines of leaders!
Choose your income!

Story Board #16

For the Trainer: Explain the incentives that are in addition to income opportunities with your company. Talk about the difference that being in this business has made to your life; display photographs, illustrations, photos and prizes that you have earned. Sell the dream! Here is what to put on the board:

Look What you Can Earn!

Trips!
International Travel!
Fun!
Incentives!
Recognition!
Prizes!

Photos!
Brochures of
current contest!
Prizes offered!

Story Board #17

For the Trainer: Explain Diamond Steps. Here is what to put on the board:

Are you ready to build a Network Marketing Business?

Do you have:

✓ Ambition?

✓ Adaptability?

✓ Resourcefulness?

✓ Determination more than anyone else you know?

✓ Faith?

✓ Patience?

✓ Poise?

✓ Confidence?

**A
T
T
I
T
U
D
E**

Are you:

✓ Enthusiastic?

✓ Coachable?

✓ Cooperative?

✓ Loyal?

✓ Industrious?

✓ Intent?

✓ Sincere?

✓ Honest?

✓ Reliable?

✓ Ready to play full out?

✓ Fired Up?

Will you:

✓ Take initiative?

✓ Practice self-control?

✓ Be alert to new ideas?

✓ Participate in team spirit?

✓ Work on your skills?

✓ Condition yourself?

Do you:
Value friendship?

DIAMOND STEPS

Story Board #18

For the Trainer: Explain that recruiting/sponsoring is the key to building a huge stable, successful, thriving business. Brainstorm ideas, let everyone think of ideas and share. Here is what to put on the board:

Brainstorm each catagory

S = Who do you know in **SALES**?

T = Who is your child's favorite **TEACHER**?

E = Who is the most **ENTHUSIASTIC** person you know?

A = Who has the most positive **ATTITUDE** you know?

M= Who do you know who needs extra **MONEY**?

Where to find business

1. Where are places to sell our products?

2. Where are places people congregate who would buy our products?

3. What kinds of groups might be interested in our services?

Story Board #19

For the Trainer: Explain that to *Go Diamond* you must seriously build the business. Here is what to put on the board:

Will _____(insert your company name here)_____work for you?

It will if you:
◆ **Take it seriously.**
◆ **Give it time and effort.**
◆ **Are self-motivated.**
◆ **Plan your day.**
◆ **Are coachable.**
◆ **Are willing to take risks.**
◆ **Tell people what you are doing.**
◆ **Ask for referrals.**
◆ **Make phone calls.**
◆ **Follow up.**
◆ **Are willing to face rejections.**
◆ **Are willing to invest in business related expenses.**
◆ **Will develop a customer base.**
◆ **Will build your successline by recruiting and selling products.**
◆ **Have a great attitude.**
◆ **Set goals for yourself, your family and your future. Know what you want to accomplish. Plan both short and long term goals.**
◆ **Plan ahead, think ahead, break large goals into small goals.**

Story Board #20

For the Trainer: Explain the benefits of your products and how easy it is to sell them. Here is what to put on the board:

Why _____(insert your company name here)_____products?

★ **Ease of explanation**

★ **Durable**

★ **Patents**

★ **Terms of company guarantee**

★ **Safe**

★ **Size of company**

★ **Product benefit**

PEOPLE WANT OUR PRODUCTS

Story Board #21

For the Trainer: Explain the business starter kit of products and/or literature that the new distributor will receive. Explain the benefits of having those products and getting started with them. Here is what to put on the board:

Your _(insert your starter kit name here)_ _____

- **Your starter kit is the quickest way to get your business started.**

- **Here is what you get in the kit:**

   (Show the kit or a brochure of the kit now)

- **Here are the benefits of having the starter kit:**

- **Heavily discounted products:_____ value for____.**

- **You can get your investment back right away by moving product when you show samples.**

- **It's your store in a box.**

- **It's like a store window; you get to set up your display as you wish.**

Story Board #22

For the Trainer: Explain the urgency of starting to build their own business now. Close by thanking all guests for coming and tell them that you and any other training leaders are available to answer any questions they might have to help them get started. Announce the next *Go Diamond* Training.
Here is what to put on the board:

Take action = get started now!

Invest in
your starter kit now!

Begin your business!

Best wishes for great success!

Welcome to the Successline!

Write your personal plan to
Go Diamond here...

_____

_____

_____

_____

_____

_____

_____

_____

_____

_____

_____

_____

_____

_____

_____

_____

_____

198

Living the Diamond Lifestyle

We started our book in Aspen, Colordo,

we worked on it some
more in Morocco,

and then some more in Spain.

And along the way we
became good friends,
playing all over the world.

To help me *Go Diamond* I will remember to:

G oal Set

O rganize for Success

D ecide To Do It

I nvest in Myself

A ttitude of Gratitude

M ake Money

O ptimize My Time

N ever Quit

D evelop My Skills

The *Go Diamond* Mystique

There is no business, no profession and no activity more noble than that of encouraging the personal growth and development of people. Diamonds are really hope coaches, for they give people visions and dreams of a hope for better life. For those of you who are Going Diamond, trust your hopes, not your fears.

Diamonds are in a class by themselves and always have been since they were first discovered years ago. Call it the *"Diamond Mystique."* The ancient Greeks revered diamonds, thinking they were splinters of stars that had fallen to Earth. In the Middle Ages, only kings and noblemen were allowed to wear diamonds. In the Victorian Age, rich businessmen showed off their wealth by buying diamond pins for themselves and diamond necklaces for their wives. *The Diamond Mystique* has not lost any of its luster over the centuries. Today, diamonds are used to commemorate special occasions, such as engagements and wedding anniversaries and to designate special achievements such as getting to the top position in your Network Marketing business.

Diamonds are forever says the advertisements for DeBeers, the world's largest miner and distributor of diamonds. Diamonds symbolize the ultimate in rank...achievement...wealth...beauty and excellence. Diamonds represent the best. The top. The pinnacle. The ultimate. Yes, *Diamonds are forever.*

How can something that so completely looks like a dull glass pebble in its natural state, be assigned such uncommon value and status? The unique combination of rarity, durability and beauty is what makes diamonds so valuable. So valuable, that every other precious metal and gem, even gold pales in comparison to diamonds. They are valuable because of the law of supply and demand. In the case of diamonds, there is a lot of demand but little supply. So, the prices remain high. If diamonds were as plentiful as gravel, they would bring the same price as gravel. Diamonds are rare. In fact, they are the rarest mineral in the entire world.

Diamonds are hard. Diamond got its name because of its extraordinary hardness. The word *"Diamond"* comes from the Greek word *adamas*, meaning *"invincible"* or *"unconquerable."* Diamonds are valuable for their beauty. No other substance has the sparkle and shine of diamonds. When light hits a polished diamond, the flat surfaces act as a mirror, reflecting the light to create a brilliant *"fire"* that is unique only to diamonds. Diamonds in their natural state are uneven and often have a dull, oily appearance. When the diamond is cut, the hidden beauty is released and it dazzles, sparkles and shines brightly, forever.

The Diamond Touch expression refers to leaders who have the know how to bring out the best in someone or some situation. They have learned the *"secrets"* of their trade, have acquired the specialized tools and have searched for, studied and learned the specialized knowledge that enabled them *to bring out the best in others.*

If anything deserves to be handled with *The Diamond Touch*, it is our relationships. They are priceless. Everything has a price. The price may be astronomical in spending your lifetime getting to the top, but it is worth it. Go for the lifestyle. The Diamond lifestyle!

Diamonds have figured out that the best way to succeed is to emphasize **OTHERS** thoughts, feelings, and values, instead of their own. Diamonds learn what others want from them and how they want it. All you really have to do to *Go Diamond,* bottom line, is to increase the value of your relationships and apply *The Diamond Touch*. Transform your distributors from being diamonds in the rough, to helping them to *Go Diamond* with you.

The day you decide to *Go Diamond*, the universe will rearrange itself to accommodate you. We have a premonition that soars on silver wings. We dream of your accomplishments and other wondrous things. We do not know beneath what sky that you will conquer fate. We only know it will be high, and we only know you will all be great! Fire up, there are *No Limits* to what you can achieve. Go for greatness, don't be average, be a champion.

Many years ago, in ancient Greece, a traveler met an old man on the road and asked him how to get to Mount Olympus. The old man, who happened to be Socrates, replied, *"If you really want to get to Mount Olympus, just make sure that every step you take is in that direction."* The moral of the story is simple. If you want to *Go Diamond;* if you want to see your dream become your reality, make sure that every step you take is in that direction. Your destiny is not a matter of chance; it is a matter of choice. Choose to *Go Diamond*; your dazzling future starts today! Fortune favors the brave. You can have reasons or results. Reasons count, results don't lie. Be brave and *Go Diamond*! You can; after all, it's simply a matter of deciding to decide! Make today be the day that you decide that you want to get, grasp, hold and enjoy having the title of Diamond after your name. It's your turn to shine!

We wish you all the very best!
Go Diamond!
Jan Ruhe and Jayne Leach
Diamonds in Network Marketing/
United States of America/United Kingdom

Feed Your Successline!

To order, contact or visit:

In the USA/Canada/Europe:
> **JR Productions**
> **300 Puppy Smith, Ste. 205-290, Aspen, CO 81611 USA**
> **Email: jrproductions@starband.net**
> **or Fax to 970-927-0112 or call us at 970-927-9380**

In the UK:
> **No Limits Publications**
> **Treberran Farm, Dingestow, Monmouth, NP25 4EA UK**
> **Email: john@qlsgroup.com**
> **or Tel/Fax to +44[0]1600 740 146**

Visit Jan's website at www.janruhe.com
Visit Jayne's website at www.jayneleach.com